Worker Activism
After Successful
Union Organizing

Worker Activism After Successful Union Organizing

Linda Markowitz

M.E. Sharpe

Armonk, New York
London, England

331.870973
M34w

Library of Congress Cataloging-in-Publication Data

Markowitz, Linda Jill.
Worker activism after successful union organizing / Linda Markowitz.
p. cm.
Includes bibliographical references and index.
ISBN 0–7656–0492–2 (hardcover : alk. paper)
1. Trade-unions—Organizing—United States. 2. Shop stewards—
United States. 3. Trade-unions—Food industry workers—Organizing—
Unites States Case studies. 4. Trade-unions—Textile workers—
Organizing—United States Case studies. I. Title.
HD6490.072U6495 2000
331.87'0973—dc21
99–23904
CIP

Printed in the United States of America

The paper used in this publication meets the minimum requirements of
American National Standard for Information Sciences—
Permanence of Paper for Printed Library Materials,
ANSI Z 39.48-1984.

∞

BM (c)   10   9   8   7   6   5   4   3   2   1

Table of Contents

Acknowledgments

First and foremost, I would like to thank all of the workers who welcomed me into their homes to talk about their experiences. Without their time and insights, I would have been unable to complete this project. Paul Rubin and Kathy Hannah proved invaluable to me. Not only did they agree to introduce me to workers, but they also read the manuscript and corrected its mistakes (of course, if there are any left, they are completely my responsibility). Paul Saba helped keep me out of jail when the company from Alabama subpoenaed my data in efforts to defeat the discrimination case brought against it by the workers. Elisabeth Clemens, Hector Delgado, Paula England, and Walter Powell read and commented on earlier drafts of the manuscript more times than they probably desired. Finally, Mark Hedley not only read the book several times, but heard me discuss it at length for four years. Thank you.

Worker Activism After Successful Union Organizing

Introduction
After the Organizing Ends

The most dynamic unions today are those whose leadership has recognized that organizing must be going on continually—both within the unions themselves and the community. Bringing out the fight is not only a matter of idealism, it's a matter of pragmatism—the survival of the labor movement is at stake (Oppenheim 1991).

When I first began my dissertation project in 1991, I intended to do a case study about the involvement of women in a local union over time. While union officials at the United Food and Commercial Workers Union welcomed me, they were unable to provide me with consistent records about their membership. Rather than turn me away, they encouraged me to participate in union activities. I spent a year in Tucson and Phoenix, Arizona, getting to know union representatives, the president, and other officials. I also attended union meetings, taking the opportunity to witness discussions about contract negotiations. At the union headquarters, I met a union representative who was sympathetic to my research interests. My informant, Mark, called me in the middle of October 1992. He was in Phoenix and told me that I must drive up there immediately; a very exciting organizing drive was underway. I drove up to Phoenix to witness the tail end of the Comprehensive Campaign at Bob's Grocery Stores.

There were about thirty organizers in town who had the job of going to the stores and collecting workers' signatures. About a dozen of the organizers were students and teachers from the Organizing Institute, a new group affiliated with the AFL-CIO that trains people to become organizers. Most of the trainees were college-age activists who, with youthful idealism, wanted to become organizers to help change what they saw as an exploitative economic system. Two of the women from the group agreed to put me up in their hotel room, and I spent a great deal of time talking with them about their experiences at the campaign.

Although everyone knew that I was a researcher, staying with these young women gave me the appearance of being a trainee. This gave me access to the private socializing of the group, allowing me to be included in conversations and debates. Plus, I was also seen as an insider within the larger organizer group and took advantage of the opportunity to attend staff meetings and ride around with the organizers as they went to the stores.

I learned immediately from the trainees that they were all bitterly disappointed with the way the Comprehensive Campaign worked. At the Organizing Institute they had learned that organizing was supposed to be a grass-roots endeavor, a chance to finally empower a group commonly without control. What they were experiencing during the campaign at Bob's Grocery Stores was the antithesis of "empowerment." Their responsibilities were to enter the stores and obtain as many employees' signatures as possible. Indeed, at the early-morning meetings, each team (two organizers) had to stand up and reveal how many cards they had procured on the previous day. People clapped enthusiastically for the teams with high numbers. Students soon were competing with each other for the highest number of signed cards. When they realized that the union was more interested in "quantity over quality," many of them felt disgusted with themselves.

Veteran grocery workers' organizers, however, were more pragmatic in their approach during the campaign. They believed that the goal of any campaign was to make the workplace union. Not until after the employees were union members was it time to educate them about the labor movement. In the meantime, veteran organizers agreed that any tactic effective in acquiring workers' signatures was legitimate. Such tactics included "exaggerating," telling workers that everyone on their shift had signed a card or that the benefits they would receive from the union were higher than they were in reality. One organizer justified "exaggerating" to me this way: "When I first started organizing, I tried to explain to people exactly what we were doing and sometimes when they heard it, they wouldn't want to sign the card. So now I don't tell them very much. It doesn't hurt them to sign the card anyway.''[1] (7)*

Clearly, a large ideological schism existed between the trainees from the Organizing Institute (including teachers) and veteran organizers from the grocery workers' union. The former camp argued that the way you organize a group has important ramifications for how workers later perceive the union, regardless of the success of the campaign. These people believed that a top-down approach would not provide workers with more power, but demonstrate what little power they had. The latter contingent, however, claimed that what was most important was providing workers with a good income and stable job and that these goals were accomplished only when the organizing campaign was successful. From their point of view, the only negative consequence was a failed campaign. These two factions had just expressed an interesting and unresolved classic debate about process versus outcome. Did any means justify the end?

I became interested in this question not only because of the theoretical implications involved, but also because of the contemporary relevance of this issue for unions. As businesses increasingly moved to avoid unions in the 1980s, unions created new organizing strategies that they hoped would bypass aggression and bolster the strength of the labor movement. The dilemma for activists was whether unions could best achieve strength by simply adding new members to the roster or by building up solidarity and activism. While I certainly cannot uncover the definitive answer to the ''means justify the end'' debate, the perceptions and actions of the workers I interviewed for this study suggest that the question is much more complex than the dichotomy presented.

Participatory Democracy in Organizing Campaigns: Process Versus Outcome

In his study of cultures of solidarity, Rick Fantasia quotes one worker's perception of her activism during an organizing campaign: '' 'It was an education in knowing ourselves, too. I think a lot of us grew a lot through it. We did things that we never thought we were

---

*The numbers following the quotes from workers and organizers correspond to the numbers I assigned to each subject.

capable of before. We went and talked to management, made our ideas clear, made our thoughts clear, our wants clear' '' (1988, 176–77). Fantasia further details the collective actions this worker, as well as her co-workers, undertook in order to challenge management's refusal to accept a union at the workplace. Studies like this one are compelling because they help to uncover the organizing strategies necessary for increasing the rank and file, and ultimately for revitalizing the labor movement. Yet union organizing research that focuses simply on the campaign period fails to consider what happens to workers after the organizing ends. For instance, what happened to this woman's enthusiasm after the union election was won? Were workers able to maintain their solidarity and activism?

The campaign period is of central focus to many labor activists and scholars because its results can be easily quantified and translated into how strong or weak the labor movement is (Hurd and McElwain 1988; AFL-CIO 1985). Indeed, businesses glorify the declining success of union organizing campaigns as evidence of labor's inevitable demise (Levitt 1993). In their pursuit to help the labor movement survive, advocates researching union organizing tend to limit their studies to one question: What campaign strategies are most likely to help organize the workplace? (Johnston 1994; Bronfenbrenner 1993; Peterson, Lee, and Finnegan 1992; Hurd and Rouse 1989; Craft and Extejt 1983).[2] Concentrating only on the campaign can clarify how to successfully mobilize workers who are potentially challenged by management resistance. Yet this narrowness of scope assumes that the organizing campaign is a single event with few ramifications for workers after the elections are complete. Given that organizing campaigns are critical in informing workers (many of whom have never had previous union interactions) about the goals and values of the labor movement, the experiences of workers during this impressionable time can potentially effect the way they feel and act towards the union after campaigns successfully end.

From the union perspective, a successful campaign is the culmination of a concerted effort to increase the membership roster of the union. After a win, organizers and workers celebrate their victory and then the organizers quickly leave town in order to initiate another challenging campaign. Yet from the workers' perspective, the campaign period is just the beginning of the union process, especially if the campaign succeeds. After a successful campaign, workers must negotiate a contract (a process that many times extends beyond the time period of the campaign) and learn how to become union members working under the contract. The campaign period, then, begins a process of educating workers about how to become union members.

Some union activists are noticing the relationship between organizing campaigns and workers' behaviors after the campaigns end. One organizer for AFSCME states about organizing strategy, "If we try to move people too quickly, even if we succeed in getting them, we won't be able to keep them. We begin the basic work of transforming the culture of the workplace, building the community . . . in order to make the union able to survive through thick and thin" (Oppenheim 1991, 49). Despite this observation, few studies consider how the events of the organizing campaign diffuse across time and place.

In this study of union organizing, I pursue how the organizing process influences workers after the campaigns end. In so doing, I examine how different levels of participation embodied within the campaign periods contribute to the ongoing education process that workers experience during their interactions with companies and unions. I focus on worker participation as the link between organizing campaigns and the time period beyond for three reasons. First, recent empirical studies on organizing campaigns suggest that participatory strategies are more likely to help unions win certification elections (Bronfenbrenner 1993). This is true even when taking into account union campaigns where companies mount expensive and well-organized operations to thwart the union. Given that unions may be more likely to adopt successful strategies, it is important to consider how participatory tactics affect workers after campaigns are over.

Second, there is a strong normative current in the United States pushing unions to become more participative (Benson 1986; Derber and Schwartz 1983). Besides the ideological incentive to give workers "voice," labor advocates also warn unions that they may no longer be competitive with businesses for workers' affections if unions remain bureaucratic while businesses begin to embrace participatory practices (Bluestone and Bluestone 1992; Heckscher 1988). Union officials also understand the necessity of conveying that unions are worker-centered institutions. A 1985 report issued by the AFL-CIO states, "[T]he labor movement must demonstrate that union representation is the best available means for working people to express their individuality on the job and their desire to control their own working lives, and that unions are democratic institutions controlled by their members'' (13). Clearly, the proposition implicit within these ideas is that once unions create ''producers'' rather than ''consumers'' of unionism, the revitalization of the labor movement is inevitable (Banks and Metzgar 1989).

Third, neocritical organizational theory suggests that participation diffuses from one organization to another (Mason 1982; Pateman 1970). In the present haste to proffer ''participation'' as the panacea to problems in all realms of society, from economic woes to community disintegration, little theoretical justification exists to link participation with financial and individual ''empowerment.'' Yet discussions in the 1970s about ''participatory democracy'' explain how types of authority structures inhibit or free participation among individuals. Theorists, like Carole Pateman, argue that inclusive decision-making provides participants with emotional and cognitive skills that are likely to diffuse across organization settings. This diffusion of activism helps establish an ongoing relationship between the time periods before and after organizing campaigns, thus setting up unionism as a process rather than a series of distinct events. While the original interest in participatory democracy emerged primarily to explain and alter political apathy, the social processes described by Pateman are general enough to explain why and how participation unfolds in many social milieus, including union organizing.

In the book, I also expand Pateman's theoretical contribution by introducing a cultural nexus to her emphasis on structure. Pateman's explanation of institutional arrangements lacks an understanding of how individuals interpret structure and, subsequently, generate meaning from it. Goffman's construct, ''frame analysis,'' suggests that individuals attempt to understand the social world by replacing complex situations with symbols. The unions in this study generated structural forms to organize workers, and, in the process, they influenced the meaning workers derived to understand the unions. Frameworks help participants to mediate their understanding of the organization and, subsequently, their cognitive and behavioral responses to it (1974).

Methodologically, I used both participant observations and formal interviews to understand how organizing strategies influenced the perceptions and actions of workers. I first observed two distinct organizing strategies in action: one with and one without a participatory democratic reputation. After my observations corroborated the reputations of the two strategies, I interviewed workers from two success-ful union campaigns. The first campaign was run by union organizers and officials. Luckily, I was able to observe the same campaign in which I interviewed workers. The regional office directed the strategy and the local organizers complied with the plan. Workers had little role except to sign union authorization cards. I compared this "top-down" strategy to a campaign run cooperatively by workers and or-ganizers. In the "bottom-up" approach, workers met daily with the organizer to build solidarity and plan events that would result in a successful union election.

A comparative case study, most obviously, allowed me to vary the key concept of interest to me, participation. However, by focusing on only two cases, I was also able to attain detailed information from workers about how the processes emergent during the campaigns later influenced the two groups. Given that my objective for this study was to discern the meaning workers gave to the strategies so that I could understand their perceptions and actions, I felt interviews were a more appropriate way to gather data than surveys. I talked to thirty workers who experienced a "top-down" organizing strategy and twenty em-ployees from a "bottom-up" campaign. I discuss how I chose the population and the samples for the interviews in the Appendix.

The Cases

In 1991, the United Food and Commercial Workers' Union (UFCW) began an organizing campaign at a large grocery chain called Bob's Grocery Stores[3] (hereafter referred to as BGS). Rather than win recog-nition the traditional way, through a National Labor Relations Board election, union officials attempted to sway the unwilling company to accept the union, a strategy called the Comprehensive Campaign. One organizer stated, "We prefer to go the voluntary recognition route because labor law the past years has leaned totally towards the em-ployer. They can appeal and litigate and stall even before you have an election." (3) The union convinced BGS to accept a collective bargain-ing agreement after three years of secretly gathering and giving nega-tive information about the company to the proper government officials.

Workers at BGS were clearly interested in being represented by a union. On three separate occasions, 65 to 85 percent of the workers signed union authorization cards. One Latina cashier stated:

> I was totally excited to see the organizers in the stores. I thought, wow, things are finally going to change. (17)

Yet the workers' excitement soon turned to disappointment. After the collective bargaining agreement was signed, employees felt more uncertain about their future than before the organizing campaign began. Workers did not understand many of the clauses the union gained for them in the contract and were frightened for their jobs when the company laid off five hundred workers and blamed it on the union. Five months after becoming a union member, the worker who was at first "totally excited" said:

> I feel that with the union, you have no rights. You have no rights, no choices. That's it. You're stuck. (17)

What transformed this cashier's excitement into feeling "stuck"?

The main goal of union officials during the BGS campaign was to convince the company to accept the union. In so doing, organizers spent most of their resources on collecting information about the company. When organizers did approach workers, it was to get them to sign union cards; the more cards employees signed, the more legitimate the union's request to represent the company seemed. In their attempts to attract card signers, organizers made promises about what the union could do for the workers. A Latina cashier admitted:

> The campaign was successful because it was all a lot of promises, and it appealed to the employees. They were scared of losing their jobs, it was almost like protection. (19)

Because organizer-worker interactions were reduced to promises of how the union would take care of the workers, BGS employees began to develop a "union as business" framework. In exchange for dues, workers assumed the union was supposed to protect their jobs, get them raises, and better their working conditions.

Employees of BGS were not given information about the organizing strategy or the collective bargaining procedure, and, when conditions did not improve, workers felt "stuck." Given that they had no idea how the union had made it into the workplace, they had little knowledge of how to get the union out. As one white stocker admitted:

> I don't know if in the history of the United States a union has ever been voted out. Once they're in, they're in. (16)

Besides incorrectly perceiving the power of unions, this stocker clearly expressed a common sentiment: Workers had little control in the union. It makes sense, then, that workers did not attempt to change their situation.

The Amalgamated Clothing and Textile Workers' Union successfully organized a small geotextile company called Geofelt Manufacturing (hereafter referred to as GM) in the spring of 1993. The union began with a Blitz, getting as many workers to sign union authorization cards as possible during a three-day period. Like the UFCW, organizers believed that, given increased business resistance towards organizing, the traditional organizing campaign was outdated. One organizer said:

> Ninety-nine percent of our elections are with the National Labor Relations Board. But lately, time has moved in the company's favor. There's constant assault by the company and the union never has a chance to get out its message. So we shorten the pre-petition period to four to five days. The entire campaign takes sixty days. (1)

After the union filed for an election at GM, organizers established a committee of a dozen active workers. In the words of one African-American employee:

> The campaign was definitely a joint effort, I would say. They couldn't organize us without help from the people and we couldn't get organized without help from them. (2)

Workers on and off the committee met daily in the organizer's motel room and planned strategy about how to win the election campaign. Six weeks after the campaign began, workers voted to allow the union to represent them.

The excitement and solidarity established during the campaign, however, soon weakened during contract negotiations. In contrast to the election process, GM employees were excluded from the negotiations between management and the union. One white technician said:

> I feel like we were screwed by the company and the union representatives during the contract talks. If they were truly concerned and interested, they would have asked questions. They would not have waited for our input, they would have come looking for it. And while they looked for some input, they didn't look for it hard enough. It was totally different than the campaign. It was the difference between day and night. (5)

Geofelt workers were more in control of their campaign than BGS employees, yet they were more disappointed with the union after their campaign ended because they were excluded from contract negotiations. Furthermore, some workers from GM tried to do something about their disappointment. Five months after the contract was signed, five workers active during the campaign tried to decertify the union. The leader of this attempt said, ''We brought the union in here; we can take them out'' (5). What happened to transform the loyalty of these GM workers?

During the campaign, the union organizer taught workers that only through their collective effort could the union win and be strong. One white technician said:

> The organizers told us the only way we could do it was by getting the help of all the workers 'cause that's what the union is, the workers. And if we don't stand together now, we'll never stand together. So we went out and talked to people, and like I said, made plans. (10)

By participating in the union campaign, workers developed a ''union as workers'' framework. Accordingly, they expected to be included in the contract talks and, furthermore, felt that any disappointment they experienced was their responsibility to alter. In this context, a movement to decertify the union makes sense.

The main difference between the BGS and GM campaigns was the amount of control over the organizing process that the unions gave the workers. Workers at GM participated during the campaign and attained self-efficacy because of it. Even after the campaign, BGS workers were unclear about how the campaign had achieved success. Yet after both campaigns, the unions excluded workers from contract negotiations. In response, BGS workers felt defeated and GM workers actively resisted their exclusion. These contrasting responses to similar contract events are comprehensible only when we consider that the workers experienced different organizing campaigns and, hence, developed different skills for interpreting events after the campaigns ended. I argue that union organizing is best conceptualized as the beginning of a process, given that what workers learn during the organizing period diffuses across time. As Mother Jones, the famous organizer of coal miners, said, ''Taking men into the union is just the kindergarten of their education and every force is against their further education'' (Jones [1925] 1972, 48). Building a strong labor movement, then, means considering the ramifications of participation even after the campaigns end.

Organization of the Book

The central focus of this book is to answer how different levels of participatory democracy incorporated during organizing campaigns influence workers' perceptions and actions after campaigns successfully end. However, I feel that, in order to cogently tackle this question, I must first discuss the political and economic context within which unions are organizing. After the legitimation of the Wagner Act, businesses, with the support of states and federal governments, increasingly began to avoid unions legally and illegally. Finally, in the 1980s, some unions developed innovative organizing strategies in order to effectively meet the challenge of business resistance. In Chapter 1, I discuss the shape and character of new organizing strategies, as well as how these innovations are a result of previous economic, government, and union policies. Historically situating union organizing allows me to avoid morally evaluating the choices that unions are making presently to reinvigorate the labor movement.

In Chapter 2, I address the theory of participatory democracy. Historically and today, labor leaders support the idea that a vibrant union movement demands active democracy. Yet Michels' early assessment in *Political Parties,* that democracy will always be supplanted by oligarchy, has shaped how labor scholars study participatory democracy within unions (Michels [1915] 1962). Michels' influence prompts researchers to ask whether democracy is possible (e.g., Stepan-Norris and Zeitlin 1996; Cornfield 1986; Lipset, Trow, and Coleman 1956), not how democracy mobilizes workers. This book is an attempt to shift the debate to its original concern within the labor movement; how does participatory democracy influence workers? In doing so, I detail the emergence of participatory democracy in the 1960s and 1970s, and address the theoretical propositions stemming from the work of Pateman (1970) and her contemporaries. I also explain how Pateman's ideas are enhanced by incorporating Goffman's (1974) cultural emphasis on personal meaning.

Workers of BGS failed to mobilize during their campaign sponsored by the grocery workers' union while GM employees actively participated in the clothing workers' campaign to organize. I attribute the different levels of activism to how the unions structured the organizing campaigns, yet there are clearly other sources of activism. I

spend Chapter 3 discussing other elements related to collective mobilization; these are labor process and organizational characteristics,
workers' demographic characteristics and workers' ideologies and attitudes towards work. I find that, although BGS and GM workers
differed with respect to the industries in which they worked, as well
as the gender and racial characteristics of the workforce, neither of
the labor forces attempted long-term or organized collective action
before the union campaigns. Indeed, the workers shared one important
characteristic that made the organizing campaigns viable at their respective workplaces: Their companies shifted from practicing friendly
human resource strategies to creating impersonal bureaucracies.

In Chapters 4 and 5, I describe the campaigns themselves. I incorporate Goffman's (1974) construct, ''frame analysis,'' to contextualize
workers' perceptions of the campaigns. During the Comprehensive
Campaign, organizers promised workers that, in exchange for union
dues, the union would provide individual workers with better benefits
and wages. These limited interactions encouraged a ''union as business'' framework, whereby workers understood and acted towards the
union as if it were a business. As a result of perceiving the union as
a business, BGS workers did not develop positive feelings towards
the union, nor did they feel efficacious. At GM, workers in the Blitz
met together on a regular basis with the organizer to discuss strategy.
The involvement of workers in the campaign encouraged an atmosphere of solidarity among co-workers that promoted a ''union as
workers'' framework; GM employees perceived and acted as if they
were the union and, ultimately, they felt their activism gave them
rights of participation within the union. Frameworks are important
vehicles not only for comprehending people's interpretation of reality,
but also for understanding their sentiments and actions as well.

I analyze, in Chapter 6, how the different democratic structures of
the campaigns influenced workers' personal meanings, feelings of
self-efficacy, and levels of activism in both the workplaces and the
unions after the campaigns ended. I study two settings after the campaigns: the contract negotiations and union life three to five months
after the contract signings. I find that while BGS and GM workers
shared similar union-controlled contract periods, their reactions to
their experiences differed. After the campaign, BGS employees still
felt bitter about the changes in their company, but remained passive
even with the union present. Indeed, they now felt powerless in two

arenas, the workplace and the union. Workers at GM, however, told two kinds of stories after the campaign: (1) in the workplace, they recounted how they voiced complaints to their managers instead of letting situations slide, and (2) in the union, a few vociferous employees vowed to take control over their local or replace it with another. I attribute workers' responses to each group's training with participatory democracy and the different cultural meanings they derived from their experiences.

In the final chapter, I review this theory to explain the different reactions workers displayed towards their workplaces and their unions. I also consider whether or not participation is the panacea that the labor movement needs to revitalize itself. While participatory democracy empowers workers, external and internal constraints prevent unions from incorporating worker-controlled strategies. These constraints cannot be ignored when discussing the potential use of participation as a tool for enhancing labor movement strength.

Given my general interest in participation and union organizing, I encourage readers not to become too focused on the unions that I have chosen to study or the strategies in and of themselves. Clearly, it is important to consider what factors may influence why some unions choose participatory strategies while others do not; however, I cannot answer this question with my data. In order to shift attention away from the unions, I will not address the unions by name; rather they will be referred to as the clothing workers' union (ACTWU) and the grocery workers' union (UFCW). Furthermore, my interest in the strategies emerges from their varying levels of participatory democracy. I could have chosen other strategies that reflected similar variations of participation. However, as I discuss in more detail in the methodological appendix, I chose the Comprehensive Campaign and the Blitz because of opportunity. A relevant question that I address in the last chapter is whether these strategies could be made more or less participatory.

1

Historical Challenges and Contemporary Innovations

Introduction

When Robert Reich became Secretary of Labor in 1992 under the Clinton administration, he vowed to create a "level playing field" between business and labor. However, he did not stop the precedent established decades before, the movement by businesses to avoid unions. Unbeknownst to many, however, unions have not been waiting passively for public guidance to renew their old vigor. Rather, some are actively engaged in constructing new organizing strategies to overcome government and business policies resistant towards unions (Shostak 1991; AFL-CIO 1985). The purpose of this chapter is twofold. First, I contextualize the legal and business climate in which unions exist. Understanding the social world in which unions interact helps one avoid morally judging the choices that unions make. Second, I describe new strategies the labor movement is implementing to attract more workers into unions. Some innovations simply involve internal growth, like merging. Others, however, include the creation of organizing strategies that try to appeal to workers who have never historically organized.

Business and Government Resistance Towards Union Organizing

Businesses in the United States have always contested union organizing (Goldfield 1987). Most companies have viewed unions as an obstacle to their "right to privacy," and government policy has historically sided with this view (Robinson 1988). For instance, in 1908 the Supreme Court agreed that union organizing strategies, such as strikes, boycotts and pickets, were unlawful uses of monopolistic and "conspiratorial" violations against businesses, and, therefore, they violated the Sherman Anti-Trust Act. Furthermore, when the federal legislature passed the National Recovery Act (NRA) in 1933, which prohibited businesses from using yellow-dog contracts, blacklisting, and company unions, the Supreme Court ruled it unconstitutional.

In 1935, the legislature passed, and the Supreme Court later upheld, the first piece of government policy that many people considered pro-labor: the National Labor Relations Act—commonly referred to as the Wagner Act.[1] Like the NRA before it, the Wagner Act prohibited businesses from interfering with workers' rights to organize, making behaviors such as blacklisting illegal. It also solidified a contractual relationship between unions and businesses, limiting negotiations around economic issues (Taplin 1990). The legitimacy that the Wagner Act supplied to the labor movement created a swell of organizing activity. As a result, in 1945, labor unions represented nearly 35 percent of private sector workers (Oppenheim 1991; Weiler 1990).

However, just as the 1935 Wagner Act resulted in a large growth in organizing activity, subsequent legislation had the opposite effect (Robinson 1988; Block and Wolkinson 1986; Cornfield 1986). Almost immediately after the federal government established the National Labor Relations Board (NLRB), individual states began passing legislation protecting businesses from the unprecedented growing power of labor unions. The federal government followed suit in 1947 with the passage of the Taft-Hartley Act.

Taft-Hartley weakened labor unions, and especially union organizing, in a number of ways. First, it prohibited the use of sympathy strikes and secondary boycotts, and allowed states the prerogative of creating right-to-work laws.[2] Second, Taft-Hartley allowed companies to ban union organizers from entering the workplace, citing the legal justification of "right to privacy," and permitted companies to use the workplace as a platform to express their ideas about unionism (Goldfield 1989; Block and Wolkinson 1986). Finally, Taft-Hartley established the "right" of workers to decertify a union and allowed replacement workers to vote on certification elections in place of striking workers. While organized labor attempted to halt the passage of this legislation, the frantic red-baiting milieu of the time outweighed the strength of unions (Goldfield 1989).

The passage of Taft-Hartley set a tone for antilabor policy and action that peaked in the 1980s, beginning with President Reagan's unprecedented firing of striking air-traffic controllers. While the National Labor Relations Board has been accused of increasingly favoring businesses in labor-management disputes since the forties (Gross 1974), Reagan's appointment of Donald Dotson (a self-proclaimed opponent to government intervention in labor issues) to head the NLRB certainly pushed the accusation into indisputable reality. Under Reagan's NLRB, employers were allowed to "interrogate" prounion employees about their union sentiments if they did not openly threaten them, and campaigns that involved "misleading campaign statements" were no longer cause to throw out election results (Sockell and Delaney 1987, 31). Yet Reagan's clear antiunion stance cannot solely be blamed for declining union strength. So far in the 1990s, the Clinton administration has done little to gain support of the labor movement; President Clinton has failed to support policy banning the replacement of striking workers and stood heartily behind the passage of NAFTA. As a result of growing antiunion sentiment within the government since the forties, businesses have had an opportunity to lawfully avoid unions.

The media also contributed to the ability of business to legitimize union avoidance. With increased international economic competition since the seventies, businesses have exploited an incredible opportunity in the media to paint themselves as the victims of "greedy" union demands. Businesses have pointed to high employee wages as the cause for their economic troubles, blinding the public to how businesses failed to reinvest in their own companies and innovate in product development (Craypo and Nissen 1993).[3] Indeed, businesses are so shrouded in the "victim" role that 45 percent of the firms in the Bureau of National Affairs 1983 personnel practices survey unabashedly admitted that being nonunion was their major labor-relations goal (Freeman and Kleiner 1990). With public sympathy and legislation on their side over the last twenty-five years, businesses have aggressively avoided becoming organized. They have avoided unions in two primary ways: by preventing union organizing campaigns and, when that fails, by ensuring that campaigns are unsuccessful.

Businesses have successfully avoided union campaigns by building new plants in nonunion areas, such as the south and overseas, or in economically devastated areas where workers can be hired cheaply (Craypo and Nissen 1993; Hathaway 1993). Cornfield and Leners (1989) show that manufacturing employment in the south increased 130 percent from 1950 to 1980, compared to 51 percent in the non-south during this same time period. Furthermore, communities in the former union strongholds of the Midwest are giving tax breaks and promises of eager workers who will not attempt to organize to companies who settle in their areas (Craypo and Nissen 1993).

Another effective strategy for businesses avoiding unions involves building employee commitment to the company by providing workplaces with wages and benefits similar to those in union shops (Cornfield 1986). For example, the "progressive" employee relations programs of IBM and Hewlett Packard are similar to those of firms with collective bargaining agreements, offering their workers the same personnel practices and compensation packages. A newer method of enhancing loyalty includes implementing participatory work programs (Kochan, Katz, and McKersie 1986). Unions are less likely to win organizing campaigns in workplaces with employee involvement programs, mainly because companies urge workers to see the union as a threat to involvement strategies rather than as an aid (Hogler and Grenier 1992; Fantasia, Clawson, and Graham 1988).

When avoiding unions is impossible, businesses implement effective tactics to reduce the likelihood that an organizing campaign will succeed. A commonly used and highly effective strategy is the hiring of "labor consulting firms" whose sole purpose is to "bring an employer the information he needs to understand why and how his employees might be organized" (Lawson 1977, 1). These firms teach businesses to defeat the union at the election by building up morale (through temporary raises or company T-shirts and other paraphernalia) and by using captive audience meetings that paint the union as an outsider interested only in the workers' money (Levitt 1993). One "reformed" union buster admits that part of the consultant's job is to make employees fearful that the union will take their jobs away. While it is illegal to threaten to move a company solely because of a union, the consultant adeptly points out the fate of other businesses that have been organized (Levitt 1993). One study estimates that presently 70 percent of employers faced with organizing drives hire consulting

firms (Bronfenbrenner 1994) and that their use by businesses has successfully prevented unions from entering the workplace (Freeman and
Kleiner 1990; Dickens 1983).

Employers also discourage organizing successes though illegal
means. Firing prounion workers during a campaign is one common
method. Freeman estimates that one in every twenty union supporters
is fired during an organizing campaign (1985). Two NLRB practices
make this strategy effective at halting union organizing efforts: (1)
There is a lengthy time period between the firing and a public hearing.
Many cases are not even heard until after the union election has occurred. This delay has the dual advantage of keeping active prounion
supporters away from the workplace during the campaign and fright-
ening workers who might consider becoming active during the campaign. (2) Even if found guilty, the company faces minimal repercus-
sions for firing a prounion worker. Commonly, courts impose only a
small fine and reinstatement of the employee (Freeman 1985).

Another illegal tactic is pushing back union election dates and the
contract signing so that businesses have additional time to discourage
workers from unionism (Sexton 1991; Moody 1988; Goldfield 1987;
Block and Wolkinson 1986; Prosten 1978). Besides having extra time
to convince employees that unions are bad for business, the company
also hopes to create frustration among employees by protracting the
campaign time period. If the union has trouble even coming into the
workplace, what hopes can it have of actually creating change for
employees? This tool has been widely employed because of both its
effectiveness and the difficulty in proving that the company has violated the legal requirement of ''bargaining in good faith.''

One result of businesses using illegal tactics to avoid unionism has
been an unprecedented leap in the number of unfair labor practices
(ULP) filed with the National Labor Relations Board. Freeman reports
that in 1980 there were four times as many ULP charges as there were
in 1960. He concludes, ''Managerial opposition to unionism, partic-
ularly illegal campaign tactics, is a major, if not *the* major, determinant
of NLRB election results'' (1985, 54).

An analysis of the determinants of waning labor organizing growth
cannot look only outside trade unions for a cause. Unions have been
accused of contributing to their decreasing ranks by neglecting aggressive avenues for organizing new members (Northrup 1991; Dickens and Leonard 1985; Freeman 1985). When union jobs in the manu-

facturing sector began to wane, unions failed to redirect their attention to the service sector. Furthermore, Northrup shows that, regardless of industry, the total number of National Labor Relation Board elections (the most common conclusion to an organizing campaign) has decreased since the fifties. In 1977, there were 10,000 election campaigns filed with the NLRB, but by 1987 this number had dropped to 3,700. Northrup claims that this lack of effort in organizing comes not because unions have been strapped for money, but rather because unions have chosen to spend their resources elsewhere (1991). Indeed, Voos finds that, although union expenditures on organizing did not decrease over time, the proportion of money spent on organizing, as opposed to all union expenditures, did decrease (1984). In the face of growing government and business resistance, then, unions failed to react defiantly by increasing their attempts to organize workers (Freeman 1985).

Contemporary Innovations in the Labor Movement

Unions, since the eighties, have begun to shift their attention towards strategies that could help them expand their numbers and, subsequently, enhance their strength (Northrup 1991; Shostak 1991; AFL-CIO 1985). The AFL-CIO has talked more about the fundamental role that organizing plays in rebuilding the labor movement and has encouraged its affiliates to develop new organizing strategies to fight back against resistant businesses (Barkin 1992; Craft and Extejt 1983). Furthermore, in 1989 the AFL-CIO helped establish the Organizing Institute, an organization whose sole function is to train interested and committed individuals to become effective union organizers (Metzgar 1991).

Even though developing new organizing strategies is the most obvious route to rebuilding the labor movement, it is only one of four approaches presently being taken by unions. I discuss the alternatives to organizing—merging, associate memberships and corporate campaigns—before describing how unions are attempting to swell union ranks by developing new organizing strategies.

With encouragement from the AFL-CIO (itself a product of merging), unions began, in the late seventies, to coalesce into bigger unions (Chaison 1986). One of the greatest reasons for unions to merge is to build membership; it is clearly easier to gain more members through absorption than through costly organizing campaigns. The added financial resources from a larger organization also allow unions to mount more effective organizing campaigns (Chatak 1991). Critics of merging point out that bigger unions often mean members have less say in the decision-making process and that attaining members through absorption is not an effective way to bolster the strength of the labor movement (Chacko 1985).

A second method of enhancing membership growth is the establishment of union "associations" to entice nonmembers into considering unions (Northrup 1991). The idea is to provide workers with services and benefits (such as medical plans and no-fee credit cards) for a small cost without forcing them to become union members. Once in the association, employees are educated about the union and encouraged to eventually become union members. Northrup fears, however, that associations will not help the labor movement since these benefits are attracting more workers who are already union members than employees who are nonmembers.

Finally, corporate campaigns are coordinated efforts by unions that attempt to convince a company to accept a union or its demands once an NLRB election has already been won. Perry (1987, iii) describes the corporate campaign as:

> A system under which pressure is placed upon not only the employer, but in addition upon stockholders, boards of directors, financial institutions which deal with the company, customers, others who have relationships with the company, and on legislators to pressure the company either to recognize unions or to agree to union demands.

As already discussed, companies can avoid unions, even after workers vote to make the workplace union, by not agreeing upon a contract. The corporate campaign exposes a side of the company it may not wish to be known publicly and encourages the company to accept the union or be subject to increased negative publicity.

For example, the United Food and Commercial Workers Union and the Service Employees International Union launched a corporate campaign against Beverly Enterprises, the largest owner of nursing homes. Their strategy was to inform various organizations for the elderly that the poor treatment of employees caused the abuse of patients. The unions hoped the groups would join together to change Beverly's nonunion policy. Another avenue these unions took was to apprise government agencies of the violations existing in the nursing homes, causing the company to pay large fines. These tactics did finally convince Beverly Enterprises to negotiate with the unions.

The corporate campaign has grown in popularity among labor practitioners over the last ten years, although no empirical evidence suggests that corporate campaigns are effective at convincing employers to accept unions (Peterson, Lee, and Finnegan 1992; Jarley and Maranto 1990; Perry 1987). What makes this new strategy attractive is the emphasis it places on coalition building. Unions get the opportunity to work with different types of community organizations, which expands their network base and broadens their scope of concern.

Moving Beyond "Traditional" Organizing Strategies

Even directly after the passage of the Wagner Act, winning an organizing campaign was not guaranteed because businesses continued opposing union recognition. Thus, as a politician plans a political campaign, unions traditionally employed carefully planned strategies to persuade workers to vote for them. The "typical"[4] campaign involved the union sending an organizer to a campaign site. The organizer was prepared to spend six months to a year building networks in the workforce and establishing ties within the community. The organizer's purpose in the community was twofold: first, to establish trust with the residents, including workers, and second, to find leaders within the workforce and the community who would advocate unionism and persuade ambivalent workers. Given business resistance, it was imperative for the union to portray itself as neither threatening nor self-serving. The lengthy period the organizer remained at the location and the networks established with key community insiders helped to establish this image. In the traditional campaign, then, unions took four steps to achieve a favorable campaign outcome: they established *trust* among the workers, *built coalitions* within the community, remained at the site for an extended *time* period and focused their energy on winning an *NLRB election* (Rostov 1948; Barbash 1948).

In order to overcome growing antiunion sentiment, as well as recruit workers with unique needs, some unions have generated creative organizing strategies that modify the "traditional" campaign. The strategies highlight or discard one or more aspects of the traditional campaign rather than abandon the model altogether. The clerical organizers focus on generating *trust* among employees; public employee unions successfully highlight building *coalitions;* the clothing workers' union compresses the *time* frame of the campaign; and the grocery workers' union, as well as the Justice for Janitors campaigns, bypasses *NLRB elections.*[5] New challenges within the workplace compelled these workers and unions to generate the new types of organizing strategies that I describe more fully below.

Historically, organizers believed that clerical workers, commonly women working in small workplaces, were unorganizable. However, successful organizing campaigns among clericals, for example those at Harvard and Yale Universities, have demonstrated that clerical workers welcome union representation (Fantasia 1988). Organizers have, however, altered their organizing strategies to appeal to the mostly female workers (Hurd 1986); they take time and establish *trust* to sway workers in the union's favor. A nice illustration is the Yale organizing campaign.

Similar to many private businesses, Yale University was strongly resistant to the organizing campaign begun by the clerical workers in 1980. The University hired a labor consulting firm to try to defeat the incipient organizing movement. A main weapon of consulting firms is to characterize the union as a third party interested merely in making money rather than in helping workers. Labor activists knew, then, that the campaign could succeed only if workers trusted the motives of the union. They established trust by refraining from "selling" the union to workers. Rather, organizers made it clear that the workers *were* the union: thus the union could not be a third party. This message was conveyed by not permitting employees to sign union authorization cards unless they were definitely for the union *and* unless they were willing to become active in the campaign. The result, as one Yale clerical attests, is " 'building a strong democratic structure . . . This structure will guarantee that this is *our* union' " (Hurd 1986, 8). In allowing employees to shape their own labor organization, unions permit historically unorganized workers to develop trust in the labor movement.

The membership rate in public sector unions began to grow exponentially in the 1960s, and Johnston (1994) argues that part of their growth is attributable to new organizing strategies. The public sphere's unique economic situation made traditional market-based organizing strategies untenable. Unlike private sector unions, where organizing tends to be localized within one labor market position, public sector unions cross many occupational boundaries. In order to bridge the myriad interests within various positions, public employees *build coalitions* within the political-bureaucratic organization, as well as among the clients that they serve. So, for instance, San Jose clerical workers at the library and City Hall created alliances around the issue of comparable worth, and these two groups established a coalition with the janitors, whom they promised to support in their conflicts with the city. Coalition-building functioned to bolster the strength of worker groups struggling within the same political-bureaucratic organization. Johnston further notes that public employees refrained from appealing to employers on narrow economic interests. Rather, by framing their interest in terms of the "public good," they achieved stronger coalitions with clients and other public employees.

Service employees, especially government employees, have an advantage during organizing campaigns: employers cannot threaten to move their business overseas. However, in capital-intensive industries, such as the textile industry, businesses have been known to move locations overnight. The Amalgamated Clothing and Textile Workers Union (now UNITE) developed the Blitz strategy to overcome this disadvantage. The Blitz strategy singles out the *time* factor to make the organizing campaign successful. Time is compressed in two ways: First, the union collects workers' signatures on union authorization cards and files a petition for an election before the targeted company even knows the union has begun an organizing campaign. This is done through intensive house calling by paid and volunteer organizers in a period of three to four days. Second, the union compresses the time frame of the campaign period to six weeks rather than six months or longer. As one organizer I interviewed claims:

> The purpose of the Blitz is to compress the time frame of the election procedure. Strength is highest right after the Blitz because the company doesn't know the union is in town yet. The old way of campaigning is bad because if the company gets to the workers before the union, the company has the power. They can create fear . . . fear of the plant closing, strikes, dues and firings. (5)

After an election, a petition is filed with the NLRB. Paid organizers remain at the workplace during the six-week process period and create committees as in the traditional campaign, teaching workers to organize their co-workers so that the campaign rests in the hands of a motivated workforce (Simmons 1994). Thus, the difference between the new and the old campaign is that the Blitz does not allow the company enough time to build an effective antiunion offensive.

Given that companies are successfully avoiding union elections through various means, such as hiring labor consulting firms, some unions have decided to organize without an NLRB election. Instead, unions attempt to convince the employer to recognize the union. The issue is how to sway the company to accept the union without an election. Two unions have developed different methods for achieving the same goal, *bypassing an NLRB election.*

The United Food and Commercial Workers' Union organizes both service and manufacturing workers and needed an organizing strategy that juggled the demands of workers in both markets—hence, the Comprehensive Campaign. The Comprehensive Campaign eludes business resistance by *avoiding an NLRB union election.* The main thrust of the Comprehensive Campaign is to gather information about the company, such as Equal Employment Opportunity Commission and Wage and Hour violations, and to convince the unwilling company to recognize the union. The Comprehensive Campaign differs from the already discussed corporate campaign in that the UFCW's strategy is used to organize a workplace rather than to attain a first contract. The Comprehensive Campaign does not use speed as a strategy, but rather unflattering information collected by organizers about the company. In the words of one organizer I interviewed:

> Those laws [Wagner and NLRA], especially over the last twelve years, have just lost all their teeth. Companies have pretty much lost their respect for workers' right to organize. Blatant harassment, things like that can go on. There are no punitive damages or anything. So as a result of that, we look to other strategies. We do extensive research and make sure they're doing their job working under the guidelines of the law, and if they're not, we let certain people know about it. (2)

In the Comprehensive Campaign, workers play a less crucial role in organizing the workplace than organizers because the focus of the campaign for organizers is on coordinated data gathering rather than on worker education. It is still necessary to obtain a majority of workers' signatures so that the company can be recognized as union. Yet organizers obtain signatures by promising workers economic advantages in exchange for union dues.

Since the seventies, janitors are unlikely to be hired directly by an employer. Instead, janitors are likely to be employed by contracting services who sell the janitors' labor to companies (Howley 1990). Contracting services with a unionized workforce have difficulty placing workers because companies can easily hire cheaper labor with nonunionized contractors. The Service International Employees Union, then, realized that to organize janitors it must organize contractors citywide. The union has successfully done so using the well-known Justice-for-Janitors campaigns (J4J). J4J campaigns build on the idea that successfully mobilizing isolated workers involves *avoiding NLRB elections*. Union officials learn as much as they can about the businesses they are organizing; organizers build coalitions with sympathetic organizations, like churches and communities; and union supporters publicize the negative information they collect about the companies (Waldinger et al. 1997; Hurd and Rouse 1989). Like the UFCW's Comprehensive Campaign, the union centralizes the control of strategy to ensure how information is collected and disseminated (Waldinger et al.). However, J4J campaigns also enlist employee support. During the campaigns, employees leaflet, hold press conferences, and attend public rallies, all with the intention of educating the public about what the J4J is and what its goals are. Activists believe that if the public is sympathetic to their aims and willing to join forces with the service workers, then contractors will have a more difficult time ignoring the needs of their workers.

All the innovative organizing strategies discussed above differ in the level of participation they foster among the rank and file. The Blitz and clerical workers' campaigns revolve around motivating workers to establish the tenor of campaign success. The Comprehensive Campaign relies more heavily on regional and national union leaders to direct the organization and completion of the organizing drive. The J4J and public workers' campaigns involve an equally shared combination of both top-down and bottom-up strategies. Yet all the new organizing strategies embody one theme: how to organize workers in challenging legal and business environments.

Conclusion

The increasing regulations placed upon labor since the Wagner Act have prevented unions from being successful with conventional organizing strategies. Some unions are attempting to bypass antiunion sentiment by creating innovative strategies. What differentiates the

Comprehensive Campaign and the Blitz is not how novel they are, but how they vary in the level of participation they solicit from workers during organizing drives. In the next chapter, I use the theory of participatory democracy to explain how this difference in participation yields considerable variation among workers' responses towards unions and the workplaces after the campaigns end.

2

Participatory Democracy: Its Possibilities and Consequences

Introduction

In his introduction to Robert Michels' *Political Parties,* Seymour Lipset writes, "Democracy in the sense of a system of decision-making in which all members or citizens play an active role in the continuous process is inherently impossible" ([1915] 1962, 34). With this sentence, Lipset not only repudiates the existence of participatory democracy, but narrows the debate about democracy within the industrial relations literature. Lipset's concession to Michels' "iron law of oligarchy" renders democracy suspect, demanding explanation. Labor scholars accepting the challenge to study democracy, then, tend to limit their questions to whether or not democracy is possible and, if so, what type of democracy is actually feasible (Stepan-Norris and Zeitlin 1996; Cornfield 1986; Rothschild and Whitt 1986; Lipset, Trow, and Coleman 1956; Gouldner 1954).

The theoretical debate about whether or not democracy is possible belies a normative push towards democracy that exists, and has always existed, within parts of the labor movement. Radical labor activists and scholars see participatory democracy as a means to an end, the end being a dynamic workforce in control of its own destiny (Voss 1993; Rothschild and Whitt 1986; Saposs 1971; Pateman 1970). The idea, generally, is that if workers are given control over decision-making, they will become active members of society. Thus, many of the studies that attempt to invalidate Michels' "iron law" stem from an ideological perspective on the positive influences of active democracy. The irony is that the question that often remains neglected is also the one generated by the normative attraction to participative decision-making: Does organizational democracy really matter in the lives of participants? Does participatory democracy actually create an active workforce?

In this chapter, I examine how Michels' understanding of oligarchy has framed the questions scholars tend to ask about democracy. I also discuss the normative current that is now bringing democracy to the forefront of the labor movement. Finally, I discuss the emergence of the participatory theory of democracy, articulated by Carole Pateman in 1970, and my theoretical contribution to Pateman's thesis. Pateman's argument is purely structural, linking institutional arrangements to individual behavior. I expand Pateman's analysis of structure by incorporating the way cultural meaning helps individuals negotiate their responses to situations. I argue that Goffman's construct, "frame analysis," helps researchers understand how participants generate meaning from organizations and, subsequently, respond cognitively and behaviorally to them (1974).

Contested Ideas About Participatory Democracy in the Unites States Labor Movement

Since Michels' description of the inevitable progression towards oligarchy within organizations ([1915] 1962), scholars have been concerned with the potentiality of democracy. Michels' well-known argument claims that leaders become entrenched within organizations because they enjoy power, are better at utilizing power and, most importantly, have the necessary technical information for maintaining power. The attempt by leaders to maintain control over the organization renders democracy impossible and eventually leads to an authoritarian regime. Michels' argument is notable not only because he aptly describes the state of many United States unions and other organizations, but also because his vision has defined (and still defines) the way union democracy is analyzed by labor scholars.[1] Advocates of Michels' argument corroborate their perspective with examples of the ossification of bureaucracy within seemingly radical organizations. On the other hand, advocates of democracy pursue empirical studies that describe the necessary mechanisms allowing for the transcendence of oligarchy.[2]

The attention given to the "iron law of oligarchy" within the industrial relations literature stems from the shared belief that, while oligarchy may or may not be inevitable, democracy certainly is preferable. Democracy is favored for two reasons: efficiency and moral superiority. The main purpose of labor unions, organized around contractualism, is to provide workers with the goods they demand from their employer in exchange for union dues. Many labor scholars claim that democracy is the most efficient system to deliver the goods to workers (Strauss 1991; Benson 1986; Lipset, Trow, and Coleman 1956; Herberg 1943). George Strauss suggests that "democracy increases union effectiveness in representing members' interests and in mobilizing these members to support its collective bargaining objectives" (1991, 201). In this view, democracy is merely an instrumental tool used to ensure that workers are getting what they paid for when they became union members.

Besides delivering the goods to workers, democracy is also shrouded in an (often implicitly) culturally agreed-upon moral superiority (Strauss 1991; AFL-CIO 1985; Gouldner 1954). Democracy is a good in and of itself. Herman Benson, a long-time proponent of union democracy, writes:

> By depending upon democracy to mobilize the power of numbers against the power of accumulated wealth, it stimulates the aspirations of workers for dignity and self-respect even while it strives to achieve the most down-to-earth demands. (1986, 359)

Benson further argues that precisely because democracy is morally superior to other forms of government, bureaucracy is inherently unstable and will always be challenged by the rank and file.

Historically, labor scholars have claimed that both workers' passiveness and organizational "maturity" prevented participatory democracy from becoming a reality in labor unions (Lester 1958; Herberg 1943). Herberg, for instance, gave voice to the popular belief that United States workers are exceptionally apathetic and unwilling to challenge conventionalism. He says, "As long as things go well, the average union member doesn't want self-government, and is annoyed and resentful when an attempt is made to force its responsibilities upon him. What he wants is protection and service, his money's worth for his dues" (412). Richard Lester's influential book, *As Unions Mature* (1958), describes how, even if the rank and file desire participation, unions inevitably grow into centralized bodies with regulated governments and decreased militancy.

The problem with many of these arguments, however, is that they describe the state of most unions rather than provide a theoretical context explaining why unions exist without participatory members and structures.[3] Furthermore, given the present emphasis scholars place on participatory democracy, it is interesting that the quest for participatory democracy and its positive influences on workers is still considered too utopian to be worthy of study. Recently, however, the labor movement is reexamining its historical attraction to participatory democracy.

A century after business unionism began to flourish, the AFL-CIO is questioning the approach that, at first, allowed it to survive. Labor leaders and scholars are now asking if the rigidity of contract unionism is hindering the labor movement, given that many companies are using strategies (if only rhetorical: see Parker and Slaughter 1988) of participation (Heckscher 1988; AFL-CIO 1985; Aronowitz 1983). In a 1988 conference sponsored by the AFL-CIO's organizing department, participants questioned the traditional style of "servicing model of unionism." The "servicing model" embodies the passive worker who merely pays dues to receive services from the union. Instead, conference participants proposed an "organizing model of unionism" in which workers are active in the decisions that affect their lives. The conference manual states, "Many local union leaders are finding that using an 'organizing model'—involving the members in solutions—results in a higher degree of organization and success" (quoted in Oppenheim 1991). The organizing model, the manual suggests, involves motivating workers to become active, which subsequently leads to worker empowerment.

Taking into account the AFL-CIO's recent attention to participatory democracy, the Midwest Center for Labor Research dedicated an entire issue of *Labor Research Review* to how unions are implementing the "organizing model" of unionism. The stories in the issue recount how particular locals have used "day-to-day" unionism to keep workers involved and the union strong. For instance, one case involves the Portland Communication Workers of America (CWA) local. The CWA leadership called a strike in 1983 after failing to agree upon a contract with management. The call for a strike deeply angered the rank and file because they had little knowledge why a strike was necessary and had no say in the decision to strike. In 1989, the union changed strategies. Rather than impose a strike on the local, it gave workers the information it had about the company and asked them to get involved in decision-making about strategy for contract negotiations. The result was that when the company saw the organization of workers before the contract negotiations even began, it relented on many of the demands during the negotiations (Butler 1991).

While the stories in the *Labor Research Review* are descriptive and compelling, they do not provide a systematic study of the issue's basic thesis: participatory unions create active members. Because the cases discussed in this book vary in how much participatory democracy exists within the union campaigns, they allow a careful analysis of what can result from different union strategies. Furthermore, I place participatory democracy in a theoretical context that allows a more nuanced view of participation, a view that corroborates some of the positive consequences for involving workers while also witnessing some problems as well.

Emergence of Participatory Theory of Democracy in the 1960s and 1970s

The civil rights movement helped establish a renewed interest in activism that expanded well beyond the African-American community. Environmentalists, protesters against the Vietnam War and many women also became critical of the political system from which they felt excluded. Many of these groups simply demanded new "rights" so that they could participate equally with wealthy, white men. Yet some activists and academics questioned whether the institution of representational democracy could truly create a free society. During this time of critical examination, a swell of participatory organizations occurred in communities, schools and workplaces (Rothschild and Whitt 1986). Furthermore, radical academics, many of them political scientists, challenged conventional political philosophies that justified exclusion among the citizenry (Pateman 1970; Bachrach 1967; Walker 1966). They argued against Schumpeter's notion of democracy, that it is merely the most efficient method of choosing leaders (1942), and argued instead that democracy should be a process meant to attain justice. In establishing a justification for participatory democracy, academics felt it was necessary to critique the intellectual roots legitimizing representational democracy. Only then could they make claims about alternative political realities.

Assumptions about human nature are at the heart of the debate between representational and participatory democracy. The ideas embodying representational democracy stem directly from classical liberal notions about human nature as egoistic and acquisitive. In the eighteenth century, Bentham ([1823] 1948) and Locke (1777), for example, argued that limiting the role of citizens in government to merely voting upon elected representatives is the ideal form of democracy, given that humans are naturally selfish and wish to maximize self-gain in the private spheres of work and family. This constrained participatory role of citizens is viewed positively because it enables people to spend the majority of time fulfilling their acquisitive natures. When conflicts inevitably arise between individuals maximizing their interest, the state intercedes as a mediator to maintain peace between the opposing parties. The political realm, then, is reduced to a regulatory function.

Another assumption shared by supporters of representational democracy comes from more contemporary philosophers such as Mosca (1939) and Sartori (1965). They argue that limiting the role of the average citizen in politics is justifiable, given that a natural division exists among humans into two categories: leaders and the led. In every society, argues Sartori, there are a handful of people possessing the skills necessary to govern. A ruling elite does not contradict democracy since its presence is ubiquitous and thus "can be neither pro- nor anti-democracy" (112). Both Mosca and Sartori believe that because of the intellectual frailties possessed by the led, a ruling elite is functional in maintaining stability in democracy. This implies that the apathy exhibited by most citizens is a positive feature of representational democracy rather than a negative one.

Advocates of participatory democracy suggest that classical liberal theorists assume human nature is static, failing to consider how human desires are shaped by socio-historical experiences (Mason 1982; Pateman 1970; Bachrach 1967; Walker 1966). The participatory theory of democracy is grounded in the belief that human nature is dynamic and that people learn to respond to their environment simply by involving themselves in the daily activities required of them. Given that human nature is learned, participation could just as easily be realized as indifference. Following from this logic, selfishness is a value gained through interacting within society rather than some inherent quality with which we are all born.

Given that people are highly adaptable, Pateman and others claim that levels of activism witnessed within society are a result of structural rules. They argue that participants in a representational democracy react to the system apathetically because the rules prohibit activism. Apathy derives, first, from the fact that political life is separate from other spheres and, second, from the reduction of participation to voting rather than active decision-making. Supporters of participatory democracy claim that, if we lived in a political system fostering participation, people would respond in kind. This means that, in their attempt to celebrate representational democracy, classical liberals merely described political indifference rather than explained it. In the same vein, asserting the naturalness of a circle of leaders amidst a sea of dispassionate others begs the central question. Do people fail to participate because they naturally follow apathetically or do they follow apathetically because their social conditions discourage them from participation?

Pateman understands that her interest in participatory democracy stems from a normative position. An active citizenry exhibits more freedom than a passive one; thus, a participatory system is superior to other types of governments. Yet she wants to disclose how the attachment to representational democracy involves its own moral claims. In arguing that limited participation in the government is positive, classical liberals (and their contemporaries) justify a political process that benefits those with power rather than society as a whole.

The Participatory Theory of Democracy

Pateman's fundamental question concerns the issue of collective participation (1970). She refutes the idea that activism is created within individuals through either their innate strengths or weaknesses. Rather, she suggests that participation is produced through the interactions of people and their organizations. She maintains, "The theory of participatory democracy is built round the central assertion that individuals and their institutions cannot be considered in isolation from one another'' (42). This relationship between structure and individual behavior is a basic sociological precept. Yet Pateman's pronouncement remains radical because she asserts it not only as a theory, but also as a potential normative strategy for transforming the political system. In her view, organizations that people interact with daily, such as the workplace, should be altered to allow them more participation so that eventually they will learn to participate in every organization, that is, the polity. In spite of her attachment to the moral imperatives of direct democracy, Pateman creates a cogent theoretical argument about participation.

As social beings, humans learn quickly the rules of an organization and adapt to them either by necessity or force. In authoritarian organizations, for example, individuals are prevented from receiving information about important matters and, thus, from sharing in decision-making. However, when people are given the necessary information about issues and are structurally incorporated into the decision-making process, they learn how to participate. In the theory of participatory democracy, then, the main function of participation is to educate people how to become active (Bachrach and Botwinick 1992; Mason 1982; Pateman 1970). Pateman quotes J.S. Mill as saying, "We do not learn to read or write, to ride or swim, by being merely told how to do it, but by doing it" (31). Following this analogy, people learn how to participate through participation.

Advocates of the theory of participatory democracy further assert that in the process of participating people gain psychological benefits and, even more importantly, learn skills that allow them to diffuse their activism to other organizations or movements—what Pateman calls "the spillover effect." Pateman argues that we prefer activism over passivity because of a natural desire to be in control of our destiny.[4] However, the reason we do not see participants in oligarchic settings demanding participation is that they do not have the necessary skills learned by participating in a democratic organization. Indeed, Pateman claims that activism, once instituted within a democratic organization, is self-perpetuating, not only because activists enjoy participating,[5] but also because activists possess the skills that allow them to participate.

Advocates of participatory democracy suggest that two types of skills are necessary before a diffusion of activism is likely to occur. The first is a set of cognitive skills; the second set of skills is emotionally based (Barber 1984; Mason 1982; Pateman 1970). Cognitive skills embody the organizational knowledge that an individual needs to engage in problem-solving. These tools allow someone to recognize a problem and then to help redress it. Cognitive skills can be both general and specific. General tools of participation can easily cross one organizational setting to another. Examples of general skills would be listening, conflict resolution, group cohesiveness and comprehension. In order to develop general skills, one needs experience making decisions. In hierarchical work organizations, general skills are associated with management because this group is given the information and power necessary to develop them.[6]

Specific cognitive tools are more difficult to transfer across places because they apply to knowledge gained from completing particular tasks that may not have relevance in other settings. Despite their specificity, these skills are crucial for participation within the organization. One example of a specific skill would be the knowledge embodied in establishing a union election date. To have an election, one must first know that policy requires applying to the National Labor Relations Board, collecting the requisite 30 percent of workers' signatures, and establishing a certification election date. Clearly, even before individuals are able to negotiate conflict and make decisions about the organizing campaign, someone must know how to establish a campaign. Workers in conventional workplaces are more likely to have specific skills than general ones because they lack the opportunity to establish information and exercise power within the organization.

In addition to these cognitive skills, self-efficacy is the emotional component that also ensures the diffusion of activism. Self-efficacy is the belief that one's actions contribute to the success of an organization. Until participants feel that their actions matter, they are unlikely to attempt action. Self-efficacy is created through the process of participating, as individuals not only learn the general and specific cognitive skills that allow participation to occur in other settings, but also develop the psychological motivation to act. Since the participatory theory of democracy assumes that people enjoy having control over their own fate, workers who possess both cognitive and emotional skills are likely to diffuse activism to other movements or organizations.

In order to establish an enduring and wide-range diffusion of activism, proponents of participatory democracy suggest participation must occur first in the workplace. Work is viewed as the logical training ground for a participatory society, given that adults experience many of their interactions within this organization. Mason states, "If we believe that human experience has any effect upon the lives of individuals, we cannot disregard an activity that occupies as much as one third of an individual's conscious life'' (1982, 103). Regardless of the organization or movement in which the participation is practiced, however, the effects of a participatory structure should be evident. For example, workers active in an organizing drive should develop self-efficacy and diffuse activism. These effects will not be as wide-ranging or enduring as employment-related effects, however, because organizing campaigns are often of short duration compared to work.

Empirical studies support many of the claims that follow from the participatory theory of democracy. The most basic idea, that participation provides increased satisfaction and commitment to an organization, is thoroughly studied in the organization literature. Organizational theorists are interested in the link between participation and satisfaction mainly as it relates to productivity. Findings indicate that giving workers even minimal amounts of decision-making power increases their positive feelings and attachments to the workplace (Lincoln and Kalleberg 1990; Mowday, Porter, and Steers 1982; Blumberg 1968). Furthermore, only a small increase in decision-making power enhances workers' feeling of self-efficacy (Greenberg 1986; Pateman 1970). Yet the diffusion of activism is what interests most social scientists. Does worker involvement translate into political activism? The literature suggests an affirmative response to this question. People with a high socioeconomic status (and a correlated higher level of efficacy) are more likely to be politically active than other groups (Zald and McCarthy 1987). More compelling are the findings about workers in participatory business settings. Studies of the plywood industry show that workers in cooperatives are more likely to participate politically than workers in conventionally owned companies (Greenberg 1986; Elden 1981).

An important similarity between many of the empirical studies testing the participatory theory of democracy is that they focus on the workplace as the site of inquiry, and with good reason. Pateman and others are morally attached to the outcomes fostered by participatory democracy at the workplace. However, because researchers focus their energies on wide-range change and assume that such change will be generated from participation at work, they fail to test how their ideas translate into organizations besides the workplace. How does participatory democracy within union organizing affect workers? Does a diffusion of activism take place? If so, where? Answering these questions not only provides us with practical information that can be shared within the labor movement, but helps to clarify how generalizable Pateman's claims are.

I want to discuss briefly one idea presented by advocates of participatory democracy that I find problematic. The goal of participatory democracy is the self-expression and self-development of its members. Yet proponents imply that this individual freedom translates into the collective good. Participatory democracy, then, not only frees individuals from subjugation of their true desires, but it also benefits the entire community by replacing self-interest (fostered within capitalism) with group solidarity. Pateman (1970) and Mason suggest that individualist values will change simply by implementing participatory democracy. Mason states:

> An important part of active life is involvement in the various groups that constitute the network of an individual's interactions with other people. This ties the individual closely to other individuals as part of human groupings and, in the process, gives birth to an alternative set of values. (1982, 23)

This statement clearly assumes that inclusive decision-making creates individuals who share a spirit of solidarity. However, I question that participatory democracy is sufficient for generating a collectivist ideology.

A capitalist economy, regardless of how the workplace is organized, encourages individuals to put their own self-interest above that of the collective. At times, the collective good may be the most efficient method to attain individual gains; at such times, solidarity in group decision-making may be evident. However, the ethos of capitalism makes it likely that workers will worry about their own survival first during times of conflict. Greenberg considers the same issue when his study of plywood cooperatives does not support the connection between collective decision-making and worker solidarity. He asks, ''Why should one expect that collective decision making in enterprises whose survival depends on the accumulation of profits in the marketplace can be based upon or produce anything other than a concern for self interest?'' (1986, 132). Given that the end of shared decision-making within capitalism is individual profit, there is little motivation for people to develop concern for the welfare of the collective.

Those interested in participatory democracy as an ideology tend also to reject a capitalist ethos for a cooperative one. When such people create an alternative organization, they are already more likely to maintain a collectivist attitude (Rothschild and Whitt 1986). However, when people come together solely to financially benefit themselves as individuals, which Greenberg finds in his study, shared decision-making will not necessarily produce a collective consciousness. Thus, the formation of a collective consciousness does not naturally flow from collective decision-making.

Participatory Democracy and Goffman's "Frame Analysis"

Pateman's explanation of institutional arrangements lacks an understanding of how individuals interpret structure and, subsequently, react to it. Rather than link structure directly to ideology, I argue that the influence of structure on individual behavior is mediated through the personal meaning that organizational participants attach to the structures. Goffman's construct "frame analysis" (1974), then, is the cultural nexus to Pateman's emphasis on structure.

"Frame analysis" embodies the idea that individuals attempt to understand the social world by replacing complex situations with representative symbols. They then act in accordance with their perceived frameworks. Thus, actions cannot fully be understood by uncovering objective reality. Rather, actions emerge from the way people attach symbols to situations and transform their feelings and images into behavior. Understanding people's frameworks, then, is important not only for comprehending people's interpretation of reality, but also for understanding their sentiments and actions.

For some time, social movement scholars have been focused on how meaning shapes actions among individuals (Gamson 1992; Snow et al. 1986). For instance, Gamson suggests that collective mobilization is embedded within the cultural frames that people are exposed to through popular culture, as well as through personal experiences. Snow and his coauthors contend that participation is linked to how congruent the beliefs and goals of social movement organizations are with the interests, values and beliefs of individuals. I propose that meaning further accrues from the institutional arrangements of organizations.

The structural forms taken by movement organizations shape the interactions and relationships among participants and, subsequently, generate meaning about the organization itself. The frames participants invoke to understand the organization thus influence, first, how participants interpret their roles within organizations and, second, how participants are motivated to act within organizations.

By bridging the participatory theory of democracy and frame analysis, I expand Pateman's analysis of structure by incorporating the way cultural meaning helps negotiate individuals' responses to their situations. I contend that frameworks help organizational participants mediate their understanding of the organization and, consequently, their responses to it.

Defining Participatory Democracy

Even though I have not yet defined participatory democracy, many readers may already be familiar with the relationships I have so far described. Indeed, it seems that theorists are more comfortable agreeing how participatory democracy influences individuals than generating a consistent theoretical or empirical definition of it (Bachrach and Botwinick 1992; Mason 1982; Bernstein 1976; Cook and Morgan 1971; Pateman 1970). However, there are three basic elements in an organization or movement based on participatory democracy that all theorists consider: (1) shared information, (2) open communication, and (3) common decision-making. Each of these elements builds on the prior one; an organization with common decision-making necessarily has both open communication and shared information.

Shared information exists when all relevant details about the organization or movement are supplied to the members. People need to know not only what issues are being discussed, but also how to evaluate the issues. Bernstein states, "[W]orkers cannot be influential in decision-making if control over their information is left to someone else" (1976, 69). In the workplace, management should disclose to workers information ranging from safety issues to investment decisions. Disclosing information is a challenge for capitalist companies since workers and owners often have conflicting interests about company goals. In an organizing campaign, however, organizers and workers share the same goal: they both are working to organize the workplace. This makes the sharing of information more likely. Shared information in an organizing campaign, then, means that all participants understand what the goal of the campaign is, know who is involved in attaining the goal, and are aware of the means being used to attain the goal.

Giving people access to information may mean very little, however, unless they can communicate openly with each other about the details under discussion. Open communication entails the sharing of information. More than that, however, it allows free discussion about the information so that all participants are aware of the issues involved and understand how each individual perceives the decisions to be made. Barber proposes, "The objective is not to canvass opinion or to take a straw poll, but to catalyze discussion and to nurture empathetic forms of reasoning" (1984, 289). The act of communicating, then, provides a forum for discussion, not for individual soapboxes. Open communication is often thought of as inefficient in capitalist organizations because discussions can take extended periods of time. Yet, sometimes, protracted conferences are necessary so that members understand everyone's view. In an organizing campaign, open communication means that participants have a place to discuss the goal, are allowed to disagree about the means of attaining the goal, and have the opportunity to voice new issues and concerns about the goal.

Common decision-making is at the heart of participatory democracy. The ability for everybody to have an equal opportunity for input in decision-making separates participatory democracy from other types of governing structures. Indeed, widely shared information and open channels of communication are important only to the degree that they allow individuals the opportunity to affect decisions. Pateman states about workplace democracy, "The whole point about industrial participation is that it involves a modification, to a greater or lesser degree, of the orthodox authority structure; mainly one where decision making is the 'prerogative' of management, in which workers play no part" (1970, 68). Instituting participatory democracy in the workplace would mean a radical transformation of the way work is presently organized, which makes businesses less likely to adopt it. However, common decision-making in organizing campaigns is more plausible because workers and organizers have the same goal. An organizing campaign based on participation means that workers have equal power in deciding strategy about the goal of making the workplace union.

I think the best way to consider the concept participatory democracy, as I have defined it, is on a continuum rather than as a dichotomy. There are some organizations that are "ideal types" of participatory democratic structures. The worker collectives that Rothschild and Whitt (1986) discuss in *The Cooperative Workplace,* for example, ensure that for every issue there is equal dissemination of information, open discussion among peers, and shared decision-making. Yet these "ideal type" organizations tend to exist outside of the capitalist system, rejecting its profit motive and market bases. Furthermore, when these "ideal types" of democratic workplaces enter into relationships with capitalist enterprises, their participatory structures tend to shift (Ventriss and Pecorella 1984; Cooper 1980; Gittel 1980).

I think it is a mistake, however, to argue that, if the "ideal type" of inclusive workplace is absent, then participatory democracy does not exist (Greenberg 1986). There are some organizations that possess only some elements of a participatory democratic structure, but certainly could not be classified as oligarchic or authoritative (Mansbridge 1980; Cook and Morgan 1971; Pateman 1970). For instance, Mansbridge details town meetings in a small Vermont village at which many, but not all, citizens discuss and vote on town issues. Pateman herself discusses the distinction between "full" and "partial" participation and how these relate to the effects of participatory democracy on workers (1970, Chapter 4). Without the "ideal type" of participatory democracy, we might not expect complete societal transformation. However, if Pateman's ideas are sound, we should certainly expect to see some changes when varying levels of direct democracy exist.

At this point, it is crucial to distinguish between the continuum of participatory democracy, on the one hand, and pseudoparticipation, on the other. Participatory democracy as a continuum means that, while not all workers participate all the time, information, open communication, and shared decision-making are present at least for some members on some issues. Pseudoparticipation, however, occurs when there is no actual change in an authoritative organizational structure, but simply an alteration in the level of participation within it. For example, pseudoparticipation occurs when members take part in a group activity that has nothing to do with decision-making, are informed of a decision after it was made, or sit in on a meeting without having a say in its conclusion (Pateman 1970). Pseudoparticipation may be used as a cooptation device by those in authority rather than a legitimate goal to empower participants (Mason 1982). Indeed, many industrial relations activists and scholars view the "new" strategies of worker involvement, like total quality management, as rhetorical devices meant to control the workplace rather than provide workers with more voice (Hogler and Grenier 1992; Fantasia, Clawson, and Graham 1988; Parker and Slaughter 1988; Shaiken, Herzenberg, and Kuhn 1986). I emphasize this distinction because there are organizing campaigns, like workplaces, in which participation is used more as rhetoric than practice.

Conclusion

The enduring tradition of participatory democracy within our economy and labor movement demonstrates the importance of studying how participative authority structures influence group members. Since we are presently at a historical juncture characterized by discontented workers calling for more voice and control in their jobs (Blum 1993; Taplin 1990), issues of participation and democracy are more than theoretical concerns: they are matters of practical concern as well. The participatory theory of democracy, dovetailed with Goffman's "frame analysis," suggests that participants generate meaning through their interactions within organizational structures, and this meaning contributes to the desire and ability of workers to participate in other areas of life.

Democracy in the workplace is now a fashionable topic, with companies beginning to implement worker participation as a strategy to increase productivity (Lawler, Mohrmann, and Ledford 1992). Unions are being warned that, unless they discard the old business unionism and take issues of participatory democracy seriously, new management techniques will make labor organizations obsolete. As one scholar suggests, "Workers have little chance of controlling industry if they cannot control their own unions. Union democracy is therefore one of the chief prerequisites of industrial democracy" (Fletcher 1970, 83).

3

Conflict and Cohesion: Worker Activism Before the Organizing Campaigns

Introduction

The organizing campaigns at Bob's Grocery Stores (BGS) and Geofelt Manufacturing (GM) share a similar ending. Contracts officially established labor unions in both workplaces. The stories leading up to the denouement, however, vary. This is true despite the fact that both plots share the same cast of characters: an employer, a workforce, and a union. What makes these two campaigns distinct is not how the "stories" ended, but how the characters interacted. During the Comprehensive Campaign at BGS, union officials made little attempt to elicit collective action from the majority of employees. At GM's Blitz campaign, however, organizers maintained the integrity of worker activism. Thus, these two narratives have one obvious distinction: worker participation in the organizing campaigns.

The main thesis of this book is that worker activism experienced during organizing campaigns diffuses outside campaign settings. Therefore, in order to rule out theoretical alternatives to this thesis, I must establish that GM workers were not in a better position than BGS workers to facilitate action before the campaigns started. In this chapter, I consider traditional explanations why solidarity and, hence, activism emerge. My purpose is to show that, before the organizing campaigns began, workers from BGS and GM shared a similar level of cohesion. Neither was likely to resist managerial control through collective militancy. This is true despite the fact that the employees from BGS were mainly white females working in the grocery industry while GM workers labored in the textile industry and were racially heterogeneous and gender homogeneous. I am not trying to argue that these distinct characteristics had no effect on workers because, clearly, people are shaped by their experiences. However, I do argue that in these two cases to focus on differences in industry, gender, and race occludes the similar reactions and attitudes that BGS and GM workers shared with regards to organizational changes at their respective companies.

The Attributes of Solidarity and Activism

Before workers can collectively mobilize, they must first recognize their similarities and build solidarity. The factors that inspire cohesion among employees, then, are imperative to an understanding of worker activism (Cornfield and Hodson 1993; Hodson et al. 1993). The most common view among researchers is that solidarity is an attribute of workers or the workplace (Zetka 1992a; Chinoy 1955; Kerr and Siegel 1954). Solidarity, in this view, is constructed as a dichotomy: it either exists within a set of workers or does not. The role of the researcher, then, is to uncover the attributes that are likely to create worker cohesion and hence activism. These attributes are commonly divided into three categories: (1) labor process and organizational characteristics, (2) workers' demographic characteristics, and (3) ideologies and aspirations. I discuss how these three categories relate to the workforces at BGS and GM, integrating the fifty interviews I completed into the analyses.

Labor Process and Organizational Characteristics

Solidarity, like class consciousness, involves the idea that workers see their interests as the same and are willing to protect these interests as a group (Hodson et al. 1993). Two main organizational characteristics related to the labor process influence whether or not workers perceive their interests as unified. First, companies that structure the labor process so that employees are involved in "intensive interaction" are more likely to encourage group commitment among employees (Cornfield and Hodson 1993; Zetka 1992a and 1992b; Halle 1984). Using

archival data from the auto industry, Zetka outlines three characteristics of the labor process that enable cohesive associations among
workers; these are spatial layout, control over work pace, and coor-
dination of work groups (see also Hodson et al. 1993 and Moos 1986).
Solidarity and militancy are more likely, then, if the labor process
involves employees who work in close proximity, who control the
work pace, and who depend on rewards as a group.

Second, emotional "distance" between workers and managers is
likely to enhance cohesion among employees. For instance, forms of
control that impose constant supervision over workers invite feelings
of solidarity because they create an "us"-versus-"them" environment. For this reason, the invisibility of control sparked by bureaucracies has the contrary effect (Edwards 1979). Several other
institutional arrangements are likely to occlude "distance" and hence
harm worker solidarity. Internal labor markets, with their numerous
levels of upward mobility, create competition among workers and prevent them from viewing their situations as similar. Also human resource techniques, such as company parties and picnics, hamper
worker solidarity by breaking down the emotional barriers between
workers and managers.

In order to understand how "intense interaction" and "distance"
influenced workers at BGS and GM, I integrate a description of the
companies into an analysis of whether or not the organization of these
workplaces inspired collective action. I find that the two workplaces
shared similar levels of "intensive worker interaction." Furthermore,
both BGS and GM workers experienced a large growth in emotional
"distance" from managers before the instigation of their organizing drives.

Bob's Grocery Stores

Thirty years ago Bob Smith founded Bob's, a grocery store that
evolved into a "superstore." Superstores provide people with one-
stop shopping by incorporating specialty areas such as video rental,
pharmacies and hardware into the conventional grocery store. Indeed,
in the beginning, each store at Bob's Grocery Stores (BGS) was
equipped with separate jewelry, clothing, housewares, toy, hardware,
automotive, pharmacy, liquor and grocery sections. During this time,
the organizational structure of BGS was similar to the superstore that

Walsh described in his book, *Supermarkets Transformed* (1993). Each department was somewhat autonomous in that it had its own manager who was allowed to judge the most efficient way to order, stock and shelve the products. The store's organization was described by one white, male produce clerk who used to be in management:

> At the time, Bob's was a company where you were your own boss. You ran your own department. You were the overseer of the whole department. You were responsible for the payroll, the profit, the whole ball of wax, and they compensated you very well. (22)

Supervisors would tell their subordinates which tasks had to be done on specific days. However, the specialized knowledge possessed by employees in the various departments, as well as the control they had over their own work pace, did allow them a degree of autonomy and responsibility.

The owner of BGS tried to reduce the emotional "distance" between workers and managers in several ways. First, BGS workers were controlled by the prospects of upward mobility. The levels of management were numerous and plentiful. Besides a manager in each department, there was also an assistant manager. Then, above the department heads, there were section managers and their assistants, who oversaw the maintenance of several departments. Above the section heads were three area managers and their assistants, corresponding to the division of the store into the meat, grocery, and merchandise areas. At the top of the organizational tree were the store manager and an assistant. All in all, one store could have thirty-four managers, one for every four workers.

Furthermore, according to the workers I interviewed, BGS compensated its managers handsomely. While managers had to work sixty to eighty hours a week, they could make up to fifty thousand dollars a year. One white, male employee who had been a liquor manager said:

> I was making more than forty-thousand dollars a year, plus bonuses. I had some college behind me but most of these people didn't. That's big bucks for someone with only a high school degree. Big bucks. (28).

Second, when Bob Smith owned the store, employees felt the company was like a "family." Smith, definitely the father of this growing family, generated a warm atmosphere by making an appearance in every store at least once a month. He remembered workers' names and asked about family members. A white, female worker in the bakery department recalled:

> The working atmosphere was just so pleasant with Bob Smith. He knew the majority of the people by name and he came up and asked them how they were feeling and how their family was. Plus, he set up counseling for people with drug and alcohol problems so, if they had problems, their work wouldn't suffer. You know that attitude that I really liked. They just always seemed to be concerned. (18)

Finally, Smith further inspired good will towards the company by sponsoring annual Christmas parties—where each worker received a bonus—and by holding yearly family picnics. In each store, managers created community by holding weekly meetings where workers, one person from each department, shared successes and discussed how to improve working conditions. While Smith was at the helm, then, workers believed management was available and sincerely cared about the lives of the employees.

The situation at BGS began to shift, however, seven years before the organizing campaign when Bob Smith sold his chain to a Canadian company. The new owners decided to increase profits by lowering labor costs. The changes began slowly: stores did not replace workers after they left the company. However, three years after the change of ownership, more aggressive tactics were used to reduce labor costs, including laying off an entire layer of middle managers (area and section managers) and hundreds of clerks. Many managers were also demoted to clerk positions. Indeed, of the thirty people I interviewed, eight had been involuntarily demoted. One white, female worker who used to set up displays explained the situation dryly:

> The first time they decided to trim down their management, I was a manager. I came in one morning and they told me. Said they cut my salary more than half and then sent me clear across town. (27)

As a result of the layoffs, several of the specialty areas, such as the hardware and automotive sections, were discontinued. The jewelry, clothing and food counters were sold to another company who managed these areas within BGS. Furthermore, the specialty areas that remained were reorganized around self-service rather than customer service. As a result, workers lost their special product knowledge. Once the unique ''superstore'' in the area, BGS now appeared more like its competition within the grocery industry.

The level of "intensive interaction" among employees changed little after the new owners bought BGS. Workers within the remaining departments of sundries, grocery, stocking, and bakery still labored closely together, which enabled them to continue interacting with each other throughout the day. Furthermore, for the most part, technology was still controlled by the employees. Even though bonuses remained tied to workers' collective labor output, wages still followed individual workers.

A large schism, however, developed in the emotional "distance" between workers and managers. The human resource strategies that were so effective at establishing a "family" atmosphere under Bob Smith's ownership disappeared when the Canadian company bought the stores. There were no more picnics or Christmas parties, nor were there many visits from the upper echelon. Instead, management presented themselves as distant overseers more interested in profit than in the employees.

The reorganization at BGS altered the level of control workers had over their positions. With the layoffs, the amount of work employees needed to complete in a day increased. One white clerk in the sundries department stated that her department, which used to be given 270 hours of employee time a week, was presently being run on ninety hours. Exasperated, she asked, "You tell me how we can get the same amount of work done with less people and less hours?" (3). The time constraint made it harder for workers to control their work pace, pushing them to complete tasks quickly rather than thoughtfully. The same sundries worker said:

> I used to really have pride in making everything look perfect. So when the customers walked in they would look at something pretty. But, after, I just tried to get my work done. I still did a good job, I'm still a good worker, but I don't have the same amount of time to do things the way I want to.

The increase in work responsibility affected managers also. They were given a budget for hours and products in their areas. If all the employee hours were used up, it fell upon the shoulders of managers to make sure that items were stocked, shelved and presentable. The consequence of having "overworked" managers will become clear below when I discuss whether or not employees wished to move up in the company.

In essence, workers lost much of their autonomy. First, without time to consider how best to do the job, they were forced to do their tasks quickly. A liquor clerk, who used to be the manager for that department, stated:

> I got moved down as manager and they took away the help I had in the department. Now, I'm doing more work, 'cause I have to do the physical work besides all the manager work and I get paid seven thousand dollars a year less. I just get done what I can. The whole thing stinks! (28)

Second, managers created more rules for workers to follow. For instance, bakers and stockers were told exactly when and in what order to complete each job.

No other position, however, was more deleteriously affected by the decrease in autonomy than that of the cashiers. The job of the cashier seems fairly routine. It is the one job in a grocery store similar to "traditional" factory work in that workers are confined to one geographical area and the pace of work is influenced by a machine. One veteran white cashier who had been with the company since 1975 described the job as "basically just checking out the order, customer service, taking the money, saying 'have a nice day' and that's it" (6).

While Bob Smith owned the store, cashiers were not simply engaged in checking groceries as they were with the new owners. Cashiers previously had more autonomy in three ways. First, they were responsible for ordering and stocking the candy and cigarettes in their area, as well as the spices. One white, female cashier remembered:

> I was responsible for ordering the Schilling gravy and spices. I did inventory and I loved that job. That was my little thing and I loved it. It was always tiptop. I also did candy and cigarettes for the complete store. It was a big responsibility. And then about four years ago they took it away from us. When I asked a couple of managers about it, they were like "If you don't like your job, quit. If you don't like it here, quit." It was like they wanted me to quit! But I wrote it down in a little booklet that I started to keep. I thought, "You're not getting rid of me that fast. This is Bob's." I was top pay and I knew they wanted to get rid of me. (24)

Second, cashiers used to have control over the money for their register. At the beginning of the workday, the cashier picked up her drawer from the manager and counted the money to make sure she was starting out with a full drawer. At the end of the day, the cashier once again counted her money to make sure the transactions of the day corresponded to the transactions in the drawer. One cashier said:

> I like the single drawer system better. You were the only one checking on a drawer. At the end of the day, if your drawer came out even, it was a

real sense of accomplishment. Now with seven to eight girls on the same drawer, you never know. (6)

A final way that cashiers lost autonomy was through expanding work rules. Cashiers were told how to greet customers and expected to remind customers to present their coupons early. They were also told not to speak to other cashiers. In order to ensure that cashiers followed their script, "sneak customers" were employed by the company and sent through the lines. If a cashier didn't say the appropriate line at the appropriate time, she was written up. A college-aged, white cashier said:

> I got written up once for not saying "thank you," plus they said I was talking to another cashier, which I was . . . but I hardly ever talk to a cashier, unless it's slow. And then I try to involve the customer. Because my mom always complains, like if they're not talking to her, but if she's involved, then it's O.K. I remember when I read the report, I couldn't believe it because I always say "thanks" a lot. But maybe that day I said, "Have a great day" or something. I don't know. (9)

Cashiers were also expected to increase their output. A new rule dictated that they increase the number of items rung per minute from fifteen to twenty-four. For a short while, until cashiers protested, managers posted the number of items per minute for each cashier in the back room. Cashiers believed the emphasis on quantity greatly hampered customer service. One white, male cashier said:

> They'll be times when I'm cashiering and there will be a long line for one of the cashiers and nothing at another and I'll say, "Hey, I can help you over here," and they say, "No, I'm in Barb's line." See, they're all Barb's regulars and they wait in line to talk to Barb. And then Barb is faced with doing nineteen items per minute instead of twenty-four and they're going to write her up! Don't they understand what that is doing to us if our cashiers aren't allowed to have regulars? (7)

The transformation of BGS away from a family-oriented company to a "big business" affected employees in four general ways. First, as illustrated through the many comments above, morale among employees dropped precipitously. Veteran workers talked about how they used to feel very loyal to BGS because there was always a higher level to move up to and supportive managers. One white, male stocker said:

> I used to love coming to work in the morning. Now, I dread it. We all dread it. There's too much to do, and if we don't do it all, we get blamed for it, not management!" (10)

The baker I interviewed said the increased stress aggravated a "problem with nerves" that forced her to take a sick leave. She said:

> I haven't kept in contact with work, partly because of the stress. I just recently talked to people there and they're saying that it's worse than when I left. So I'm wondering if I really want to go back there. And I really did like my job. But there's nobody you can go to talk to about the problems 'cause they all have problems from their boss. (18)

More recent employees discussed how the high stress and low pay made it more difficult to create a "fun" work atmosphere.

Related to a drop in morale was an increase in the turnover rate. Employees of BGS, once proud of their loyalty to the store, were now looking for different jobs. Another way, then, in which BGS looked more like its competitors was a turnover rate that climbed to almost 50 percent per year. A young, female courtesy clerk who had been with the company for three years said:

> I've been with the company for a long time and I still haven't been moved up. They had all these layoffs and now they're not moving people up like they used to. So I'm looking for other work. (11)

The changes had a curious effect on worker community. Most of the employees talked about the cohesion they felt due to their loyalty to the company when Bob Smith owned the chain. However, after Smith sold the chain, the solidarity workers felt towards the company shifted to a department or a store and sometimes dissolved altogether. For instance, a white, male night stocker said:

> Our group is pretty tight. We gotta be, given we're there alone at night with all those things to do before the morning. (10)

Yet a stocker with a contrary view said:

> Sometimes I'd get called to front because the cashiers needed help. Some of the stockers got real mad at me because when I left they would have more work to do. It has created some conflict. (16)

On occasion, the solidarity among employees inspired organized and unorganized collective action. Only one year after BGS sold the chain, fifteen workers began secret meetings to discuss organizing a union. The workers were mainly from three stores, one of which I sampled for interviewing. A white, male scanning coordinator, who was part of the original campaign, remembered:

> It was one of my favorite times. We would organize and get together
> secretly and talk about our grievances. (1)

However, after only one month of meetings, managers found out about
the union attempt. They called all the participants separately into the
manager's office and told the workers that a union could potentially
harm the company and, thus, their jobs. The workers gave up their
organizing efforts for fear of losing their jobs.

Cashiers, the group most affected by the changes, discussed several
examples of informal collective resistance during the interviews. One
example already mentioned involved cashiers verbally protesting
when management publicly posted their items-per-minute. Another instance occurred several years after the Canadian company bought
BGS: management told the female cashiers to wear dress shoes to
work. One veteran white cashier recounted:

> They think that, because we're just peons, we don't know anything. One
> time they told us we had to wear dress shoes to work, like we're going to
> stand there eight hours a day in dress shoes. Well, everyone threw such a
> fit, and the next day we came in and none of us wore the shoes. Manage-
> ment pretended they didn't notice. They just took the sign down real qui-
> etly. (2)

However, collective action was more the exception than the rule.
Mostly, workers admitted, they just "griped" about the changes. In
fact, their relationships with co-workers had been reduced to "gripe
sessions." One white housewares clerk said:

> I still love the people from work. They're good people. But really, some-
> times all we do is sit together and complain. (12)

Finally, workers admitted that the primary way they resisted the negative changes within the company was by not putting their entire effort
into work. Here are some ways in which workers described this
resistance:

> *White, Female Cashier:* They take a fifteen-year cashier and they stick us
> in a cage for forty hours a week. We hate it. We all hate it. And maybe
> I'm not as fast as I used to be. Well, what do they expect? (2)
>
> *White, Male Stocker:* The Canadians, they're sucking us dry. They want
> money now. Everybody hates it. I know that we don't work as hard. I don't
> work as hard. But I'm still a good worker. I know my job. But you know,
> it's just bad for morale. (5)
>
> *White, Female Housewares Clerk:* I used to love work. I used to come in
> thirty minutes early off the clock. But now there just isn't incentive any-
> more. (12)

> *White, Female Cashier:* We used to work hard because we were working for the company. We felt like a group as a company. Now we work for our own particular store, and we're not as loyal to the front office people. I just don't think we work quite as hard because of it. (26)

Workers were always careful to point out that their work ethic had little to do with their own motivation; instead, they attributed their decreased effort to the company and its policies.

Some employees expressed sympathy for the new owners, given the competitive grocery climate they faced when they bought BGS. Yet the majority of workers, including the sympathetic ones, believed that the changes made by the Canadian company were only short-term solutions that would not improve the long-term viability of BGS. "Maybe if I had been on the business side I could see why all the cuts were necessary," said the baker I interviewed:

> But I just can't see how these changes are good for the company. Customers just aren't as loyal. I know because I'm also a customer. And I wait in line longer. And I can't find what's on ad. And I would quit shopping there if I didn't work there. (18)

One stocker more succinctly said, "They're slitting their own throats!" (5)

Employees offered two suggestions for improving conditions at the company: revive customer service and listen more to workers. First, while management was trying to force BGS into the same mold as every other grocery chain, employees perceived that the drive towards "sameness" propelled BGS downward economically. A frustrated stocker admitted:

> People want help in the stores when they go shopping. They want customer service more, and that's what made us different. We could give that to them and our business would be better, but we would have to have more people. (5)

Second, workers believed that the company should incorporate employee voices into company decision-making. Workers cited news sources and knowledge from college courses to justify why they felt employee input into the company was important. For instance, one white, male stocker said he saw a news program linking worker participation with enhanced morale. He said:

> I heard on the news recently about some machinist company that was making a lot of defective products. They found out that, when employees

had input into the company and that input was listened to, people's self-esteem went up and the defects started going way down. (4)

More importantly, workers felt that working closely with the products and customers gave them an intimate understanding of the stores and thus gave them a legitimate reason for having a voice. A Latina cashier suggested:

> If we were asked, as individuals, to give our opinions on how to improve the work environment, we could improve a lot of things. For example, they want us to move customers quickly and still ask them for their coupons and passport cards. If we had some sort of sign in the line that reminded people to have all their things ready, it would really speed things up. Plus, any basic management course teaches you that's how to make employees feel more involved. (19)

Employees agreed, then, that one simple solution to BGS's downward economic spiral was to listen more to the people running the stores.

Geofelt Manufacturing

Most people are familiar with the work process at a grocery store because they have been inside one and experienced it. Yet not many know the product manufactured at GM, much less the manner in which it is produced. Geofelt produces a polymer insulation material that is commonly used to line the bottom of landfills, keeping refuse from seeping into the earth, to lay underneath highways, preventing the formation of potholes, and to set beneath beaches, slowing down erosion.

The process of creating the insulation material involves a very sophisticated technology. On the sixth floor of the GM building, a machine melts polypropylene plastic pellets into a polymer. The melted polymer is pushed through a "free float system" down to the third floor, where it is cooled by a quench air device and turned into a solid. From the third floor, the solid travels to the second floor where it is distributed through a multitude of nozzles to create fibers. The fibers are then bonded together in a process known as "nonfilament continuous bonding," which tangles the fibers tightly to make them strong. The material is then coated with a special spray, called avivage, to make it more durable. Lastly, the final GM product is sent to the first floor where it is wound up into rolls on a winding machine.

The process must continue twenty-four hours a day because, when the machine cools, it is extremely difficult and time-consuming to clean the cooled polymer off the machine.

The job of employees who work on the product line at GM is to make sure the product is running through the machines efficiently and continuously. Some people described their position as "monitor." Others described it as "process control." These people watch the line to make sure the technology does not malfunction and the machines do not break. There are three types of workers on the product line. The first are the extruder technicians who work on the sixth floor, transferring polypropylene pellets from rail carts to the system. Because the customer has specifications that the company must meet, the extruder operators know what type of product they are making so they can properly place the materials into the machine. Of the production workers, extruder operators have the most freedom to move around. After the pellets are loaded into the system, the workers have the opportunity to walk around the plant and provide help to others in need. The lack of confinement is what extruder operators liked about their job. One white veteran of the plant stated:

> Extruder area gives you the most independence. You sorta get to know a little bit of every area 'cause you can help out wherever you're needed. (19)

Needle and dye stand operators work on the second floor. These two areas are very noisy and the technicians are required to wear protective ear plugs. The dye stand is where the solid polymer is distributed into nozzles to make fibers. The technicians must be certain that the material is distributing correctly and that the fibers do not tangle and break before they enter the needle area. The same technicians then proceed to the needle area, where they work in the most difficult and monotonous job on the line. The operators sit on a stool and stare at the needles to make sure they do not break or create any problems for the product. It is a difficult job because the technicians must catch any problem before it arises; it is monotonous because they cannot divert their eyes from the rapid needle movement for any length of time. Many technicians talked about how hard it was to remain awake in the needle area because the noise level is so high and the activity level is low. One white, male dye stand operator said:

> The work isn't physical, but the area has a very high noise level. There's nothing to do. You can't read or talk to anybody. All you do is watch. It's a mental strain just to stay alert. (13)

This employee said he was looking for other work because the isolation he experienced was not worth the benefits paid by the company.

Finally, there are the winder operators, who are the most active workers on the line. As the product leaves the line, it is quickly wound into a roll by a machine. The technicians make sure the roll is even and tightly bound. Then they place the finished product on a cart that brings it to the shipping area. The winders have the most physical jobs on the product line. One white technician recalls a shift he had in the winder area:

> The winder area, it can get really hectic. I don't envy those fellows at all. You're always running around making sure everything is just right and you just can't do it with the number of people they give you. (18)

The technicians comprise the majority of employees at GM. There are twelve on each of the two assembly lines, divided into a total of four shifts. Each shift is twelve and a quarter hours long and begins at 6:15, a.m. and p.m. Shifts meet fifteen minutes before line work with supervisors, when they find out what product they are making and are apprised of any problems. Technicians work one shift each day for two days in a row and then are off two days. Every month the night shift changes to day shift and vice versa. Employees especially like the idea of having two days off in a row, but none are happy about having to work the night shift. The night shift throws off workers' sleep patterns and makes it difficult to do anything but work. "You have to rest on night shift," explained one African-American technician:

> You need your rest because at 4:30 your eyes get so heavy. They get real heavy so that it's painful to fight sleep. I hate it. And on nights, you don't have much time to do nothing, because you work twelve hours and come home and everyone else is at work. (6)

The level of "intensive interaction" among technicians at GM is comparable to the level at BGS. First, employees within a shift must coordinate their labor in order to successfully create the final product. A mistake by the extruder operator can cause the whole operation to halt. However, while technicians are responsible for correcting the problems with the product as it moves through the line, they cannot stop the line if a problem exceeds their capability. Rather, a supervisor is informed of the trouble, and then he makes the decision to stop the line, correct the problem by himself, or ask another worker for help. The passive labels workers give themselves, "monitor" or "process control," illustrate that workers do not perceive themselves as controlling technology.

Furthermore, the positions of workers throughout the six-floored plant make it difficult for workers to labor in close proximity to one another. Even though the needle and dye stand operators have a chance to sit down close to each other, the noise level and necessary concentration make it impossible to carry on a conversation. Workers, however, manage to do some socializing on the job. Extruder and winding operators said that at times they can carry on a conversation, especially if the line goes down, and employees talk before and after their shifts. Yet workers find it problematic to interact across shifts. "You're lucky if you like the people on your shift because that's all you're gonna see," said one white technician who had been with the company for two years. "I mean, until the campaign, you might not have even met some of the other folks on the other shifts." (5)

Like the technicians, the other employees at GM also require considerable skill. The maintenance crew, seven workers, repair the machinery when it malfunctions. They have the greatest skill and receive by far the highest wage of all the factory workers (none of them joined the union after the successful organizing campaign). This group has a high level of autonomy and control over the technology. The five lab specialists test the completed product to make sure the company is making high-quality material. They labor closely in one room and have some command over the equipment; however, their efforts are not coordinated. Finally, the ten warehouse men are responsible for the product once it passes inspection and is ready to be stored. Not only do they place the material in the warehouse, but they also pick it up when a product is ordered by a customer. These workers do not labor with others and are fairly autonomous. All these positions, unlike the line employees, require traditional working hours, five days a week.

The managerial scheme at GM looks like the traditional bureaucratic, pyramid structure. In control over the entire operation, including the lab, warehouse, maintenance, and technician positions, is the plant manager. The plant manager makes sure all parts of the organization are running efficiently, and he also makes production decisions concerning what material is to be made, when and how. Each area is also headed by a manager, who is responsible for doling out work roles to his employees each day and handling any employee questions or problems. The technician area is further divided, with a supervisor overseeing both product lines and assistant supervisors in control of each of the two product lines.

The workers I interviewed claimed that they do not often see their supervisors throughout the day, although the supervisors assign jobs and help trouble-shoot. Workers did not complain too much about not seeing the supervisors around because it means they have little direct supervision when doing their jobs. Workers agreed that the job is much more enjoyable when no one is "hounding" them. Some workers even make sure that direct supervision is minimal. As one white technician explained:

> The supervisors don't hound you and mess with you too much. 'Cause when you get the men mad at you, there's a lot of things that can happen on that line. I've seen an extruder operator put water in his system just to get back at the supervisor 'cause the supervisor was hounding him. The supervisors sort of know that, so they don't hound us. (19)

Most of the employees said that supervisors watched over them their first few weeks on the job. However, as they gained experience, employees were less likely to be closely monitored.

When GM opened in 1987, with only one product line and twenty-four technicians, management attempted to reduce the emotional "distance" between managers and workers by practicing human resource techniques. First, to enhance morale and keep workers committed to the job, upper management made weekly trips to the plant to talk to workers. Second, the company sponsored periodic picnics and volleyball games, encouraging all workers to participate with their families. Finally, management created numerous skill levels that gave workers the impression that there was wide opportunity for mobility.

The high-tech machinery used at GM requires that technicians have strong skills, which are developed through on-the-job training. Commonly, an employee begins in one area, learns that area fully, and moves on to another. Corresponding to the three areas are different skill levels that the employees master in order to receive a raise. There are seventeen skill levels in all: six levels for the extruder, six for the needle and dye area, and five for the winder. One's skill level coincides with one's ability to handle problems on the line. Thus, a technician with a sixteen skill level (the highest at the plant) is able to work in all three areas and fix most problems he encounters. The rest of the positions are also divided by multiple skill levels.

Two years before the organizing campaign, a second product line was introduced in the company that ran twice as fast and produced twice as much material as the first line. The additional line heralded a new management strategy at GM. Workers felt that, with the new line, management became more concerned with quantity over quality. With this shift in concern, the "distance" between managers and workers began to grow. The company's party to welcome the new line was the last human resource attempt to create solidarity between management and workers. There were no more company-sponsored group activities and the men in "suits" stopped visiting the floor to talk to the workers.

Furthermore, despite the increased output, the same number of men were hired to run the second line as the first. Each area was staffed with four technicians, two per area per line. Almost all the technicians were upset about the introduction of the new line because it ran extremely fast, making it difficult for technicians to spot problems before they happened. The result was that GM was producing more wasted material, product that they could not sell. Unusable material meant that technicians had to stay past their twelve-and-a-quarter-hour shift to "bale waste." In addition, the problems created by the fast pace were exacerbated by not having more workers to help control the line. As at BGS, then, the shift in managerial strategy reduced the amount of control workers had over their jobs. Every employee I interviewed discussed the shortage of necessary hands and complained that work was extremely difficult because of it.

Ironically, even though workers saw less and less of the "suits," they did not blame them for the negative changes at the workplace. In fact, most of the workers insisted the president of the company was a wonderful person and speculated that he would be angry to know the way the company had been run in his absence. One African-American technician active in the organizing campaign said, "The president is a great guy. He just didn't know a lot of the things that were happening." (6)

Finally, one other problem that enhanced "distance" between workers and managers after the second line was introduced was that technicians were no longer evaluated regularly for skill level. This meant they were not receiving raises. A related issue was that employees were not getting cross-trained. Once they "maxed out" in a skill level of an area, they were unable to move up because they were forced to remain in the area they knew. Employees attributed these problems to a new manager who they felt cared more about the quantity of material produced by the second line rather than the quality-of-life of GM employees. Workers also accused the new manager of being racist. More senior workers agreed that the manager was more likely to verbally harass African-Americans and even less likely to give them raises than whites.

Like the situation at BGS, then, GM transformed from a pleasant working environment to one in which employees felt overworked and underappreciated by management. One white technician interpreted this change as the "Americanization" of the company:

> The Europeans are so much different with their type of attitude towards their work. And I think, in the beginning, I think the pride they take in their work and the workplace bled over to us Americans. I think it was good. But it seems like the more they Americanized the company, the more of an attitude that people from Geofelt felt and then we became just like every other company. (14)

This "Americanization" had three effects on the workforce. First, the turnover rate increased dramatically with the introduction of the second line. The pace and stress of work forced a 50 percent turnover rate, which, as everyone agreed, prevented employees from really learning the job and, ultimately, prevented everyone from creating a good product. Second, employee morale decreased. Most workers mentioned how proud they had been at first to work at GM given that it was one of the few high-capital industries in the area that did not involve heavy physical labor. However, as one white technician explained:

> That second line would go down, and it would be out of my hands, out of my control to keep it from going down, yet I'd still be the one blamed because. . . . And it's just so frustrating. Several times I've felt like just throwing my tools down and walking out and saying, "You know what you can do with your job!" (19)

Employees perceived that management blamed them for the new problems, which left workers angry and frustrated.

Finally, employees felt that the sense of community among the workers had been harmed. "After Line Two, the people started divid-ing," said one African-American in the shipping department:

> I guess I won't say divided, but not united. It wasn't like a night-and-day type of thing. It was just people doing their own thing. That was fine with me. I do my own thing, but I feel like if you work with somebody, if you work twelve hours a day, you have to feel some kind of relationship with them. (12)

The main reason workers expressed for not collectively resisting the negative changes at GM was that the supervisors had ultimate say over the employees' jobs, regardless of how unfair their decisions were. Many workers were silenced because the indiscriminate rule that supervisors had over them made workers fearful for their jobs.[1] One employee with the company six years said:

> 'Cause if you ain't gonna do what the supervisor says or the supervisor don't like you, you don't have a chance of getting a raise or a vacation or anything. Basically, it's really left up to the supervisor. There's some peo-ple out there that the supervisor will flat out cuss and they get away with it 'cause people don't say nothing. (19)

Thus, even though the company had a human resource manager who was supposed to listen to employees, fewer people over the years went to speak with him. One African-American technician explained:

> You'd go in the office with him and no matter what you said or how bad the supervisor was, he was always on the supervisor's side. It's that simple. If you didn't work well with a supervisor you'd get fired. (1)

While many workers did not openly resist supervisory rule, some said they quietly rebelled by not working as hard. A young, white technician remarked:

> I think the supervisor needs to think about the people on his shift first before making some quota for the company. Because without the people on the shift being happy and satisfied with what they're doing, he's not going to make that quota no matter how much he run it. If the supervisor gives you a hard time about running something, even though you're already out there trying your hardest, you're going to get the attitude of, "Well, the hell with it!" (10)

As this employee implied, morale and productivity were directly linked.

GM workers had ideas about how the workplace could change to increase their morale, despite what management thought. Like the employees from BGS, they believed the key to a healthy and productive company lay in employee participation. The workers reasoned, first, that the people doing the job knew best how to get the job done. One white technician, who had been with the company since the beginning, said that the company was losing money by not listening to workers' advice:

> I feel like there's, maybe, some bad decision-making done on the coordination of the raw material and the product we're running because some raw materials run better than others for certain applications. Sometimes I feel that the company tries to save five dollars, maybe, for instance, in running one type of material and winds up spending ten to make it run. Rather than go ahead and pay the little extra, the seven dollars for the good material, and have a good finished product, we're trying to save a dollar here and there, when they wind up losing that at the end. (14)

When I asked the technician why he did not share his ideas with management, he said, "They know what they're doing and they do it anyway." Another reason workers gave for including employees in company decision-making was that employees would work harder when they knew their input was appreciated. One African-American technician, who was trying to start his own business, said that the company treated workers like machines, and this affected how hard they worked for the company. He said:

> The better relationship you got with management, the better people will work for you. I really believe that's true. My experience at the furniture store, the relationship between the management, upper-management, sales guys and warehouse, we were like valued and it was more like a family. I had no doubt that if I asked somebody if I had a problem with the employees we could sit down and work it out. (7)

Some GM workers, like BGS employees, legitimized their discussion of participatory management by citing television news stories or books they had read. One African-American worker talked about Theory X and Theory Z:

> In the Theory X point of view, they don't think workers care anything about their jobs but money. But we do care, we want to succeed. If they had been giving us raises and treating us fairly, everything would have been fine. But they haven't done that so we had to get the union. That's where Theory Z comes in. They needed to update their thinking as far as modern styles at the work place, and we helped them out. (15)

Geofelt workers believed that the style of management the company followed after the second line was installed directly related to why a union was necessary at the workplace.

Summary

Bob Smith created a familial atmosphere by establishing social ties with employees through company parties and personal interactions. The new owners, however, soon began to resculpture the grocery stores into a more traditional shape. The shift in work organization decreased worker autonomy since fewer employees were expected to do the same amount of work. The increased demands affected the emotional ''distance'' between workers and managers. Most employees resented the changes created by the new owners. However, very few collectively mobilized against the transformation. The only instances of collective action involved a short-lived organizing campaign one year after the Canadian company bought BGS and informal resistance by cashiers. Mostly, workers resisted individually by not working as hard.

Similar to BGS, the GM company changed the organization of work by expecting fewer employees to labor more. Company parties and picnics disappeared when the second line was introduced, and workers felt overwhelmed when middle management failed to give them raises and treat them humanely. The emotional ''distance'' grew between managers and workers with the problematic introduction of Line Two and the hiring of a new manager. Even though most workers felt embittered towards the company, employees did not attempt to start a union before the organizing campaign under study. Like workers from BGS, GM employees said that they mostly resisted the changes by not putting their all into their jobs.

Workers' Demographic Characteristics

Geofelt is nestled quietly inside the wooded lands of rural Alabama in a town of three thousand. Defunct plantations and small farms surround the community. The nearest cities are a sixty-mile drive to the north or south. The small towns throughout Alabama, however, are dotted with manufacturing companies that come in search of nonunion, low-wage workers. The mostly male workforce at GM tend to live far from the plant, the average person driving thirty minutes each way from four neighboring counties. Both African-Americans and whites, who make up 45 percent and 55 percent of the workforce respectively, are attracted to the job because of the healthy benefits package the company provides, as well as the extensive periods of time off.

Bob's supermarket chain, on the other hand, exists in the heart of the largest metropolitan area in Arizona, a city with a population exceeding two million. Given that Bob's Grocery Stores are sprinkled throughout the area, workers tend to apply and work at a BGS closest to where they live. As in the larger retail industry, gender helps determine the positions workers have at BGS: women tend to be cashiers, bakers, and merchandise clerks, while men are stockers, carry-outs, and managers. The gender breakdown of positions means that women make up 60 percent of the workforce. Furthermore, the work group is mostly white (85 percent) with a small proportion of Latinos (12 percent) and African-Americans (1 percent). Clearly, the demographic distinctions between BGS and GM workers are considerable. The question at hand concerns how these differences influence the predispositions of workers from BGS and GM to engage in activism.

Historically, radical theorists have suggested that, while militancy was surely to follow from specific economic conditions, particular demographic characteristics are more closely associated with exploitation than others. Hence, the stereotypical revolutionary image is that of urban males rising up en masse to overthrow their oppressors. Marx and Engels ([1988] 1963) predicted that a revolution would occur first in urban centers where workers, living and toiling in close proximity, became aware of their collective exploitation. Furthermore, not only were men more likely to be in the labor force than women, but the social construction of men as strong, independent and fierce and women as frail mothers certainly helped to enforce the idea that men would be the leaders in activism (Lopreato and Hazelrigg 1972). Finally, their minority numbers meant that African-Americans would not dominate a revolution; however, their social discrimination and isolation certainly meant that they would disproportionately join it (Leggett 1968). Thus, thirty years ago, militancy was seen as mostly an urban, African-American and male phenomenon.

Certainly, when Marx was writing, capitalists built their industries in urban centers using racism and sexism to hire a young, white, male workforce. However, the structure of the economy and labor force has shifted dramatically since then. When companies have not switched from the production of manufacturing to service goods, they have tended to move their sites to southern, rural areas, places where workers are hired more cheaply and seen as less threatening (Cornfield and Leners 1989). Also, women now constitute almost one-half of all workers, giving them more stake in how the workplace is organized. With these changes in the economy comes a more complex understanding of how workers' demographic characteristics relate to activism.

As industries have moved from northern cities to southern towns, unionization rates have decreased. Some researchers argue that rural workers are less likely to desire unionism or engage in activism because they possess a more individualist philosophy, labeled the "mill town complex," attributable to the paternalistic organization of the plants and the lack of other employment opportunities (Zingraff and Schulman 1984; McDonald and Clelland 1984). In contrast, Kerr and Siegel (1954) propose that "isolated masses" in rural communities are more likely to produce militancy given that workers are often homogeneous groups with undifferentiated and nontransferable skills. While these two lines of research make different predictions about rural workers, their logic is consistent. The more dependent workers are on a single employer and the more differentiated workers are with regards to skill, wages, gender, and race, the less likely they will engage in militancy.

When researchers began to study women's increasing participation in the labor force, they discovered that women did not join unions at rates comparable to men. Scholars, at first, attributed women's lower activism to a lack of union interest, an indifference academics thought stemmed from women's primary role as mothers. Present studies, however, show that women are more likely than men to say that they would vote for a union if an election were to occur at their workplace (Freeman and Medoff 1984) and that female-dominated workplaces are more likely to win campaigns than male-dominated ones (57 percent versus 33 percent respectively) (AFL-CIO Department of Organizing, 1989).[2] Furthermore, case studies confirm that when women are given the chance to organize, they do act militantly in their attempts to secure a bargaining agreement (Bronfenbrenner 1993; Hurd and

McElwain 1988; Fantasia 1988; McDonald and Clelland 1984). While women's attitudes may not deter them from joining unions or acting militantly, research does confirm that the time constraints women face in juggling family and work responsibilities can prevent women from being as active as men, especially in the formal union structure (Cornfield, Filho and Chun 1990; Roby and Uttal 1988). Thus, what makes women less likely than men to be active is their responsibility in the home, not an inherent lack of interest or potential.

African-Americans established a viable community structure during the sixties' civil rights movement that encouraged activism and militancy. Academics suggest that the endurance of a culture of radicalism creates an African-American workforce more willing than whites to challenge capitalist control (Cornfield and Hodson 1993; Leggett 1968). Yet there is some debate as to what happens when a workforce is racially heterogeneous. Split labor market theory proposes that employers use racial tensions to divide the working class and prevent them from noticing their commonalities (Bonacich 1972). Some case studies support this idea (e.g., Hodson 1995). However, a meta-analysis of case studies by Hodson does not find that racially heterogeneous workplaces are less likely than racially homogeneous workplaces to experience solidarity or engage in militancy (1995). The concept of ''homogeneity'' is still important in that it emphasizes how workers must interpret their interests as similar before they will act collectively. While race, in some cases, may not be the dividing factor, the more differences there are between workers, the more difficult it is for them to act in concert.

The previous discussion suggests that geographic location, gender, and race relate to solidarity and activism in three main ways. First, workers who are reliant on one employer are less likely to mobilize. Second, time constraints, commonly experienced by women with family responsibilities, can prevent workers from participating in collective action. Third, distinct cultural and economic experiences may reduce cohesion among workers and, thus, inhibit activism. I find that, at both BGS and GM, while company dependence and family responsibilities were not an issue for most workers, employees did tend to establish social ties with co-workers who shared similar job position, gender, and race statuses.

Similarities and Differences at Bob's Grocery Stores

Workers applied at BGS, they said, mainly because it was their neighborhood grocery store and they needed work. Given that neighborhoods tend to be racially homogeneous, so were the stores. For this reason, the most important sources of cohesion among workers within their stores were gender and job position. Cashiers, mostly women, made wages comparable to the stockers, mostly men, earning as much as twelve dollars an hour for veterans. However, the bakers and merchandise clerks in housewares, toys, and photo/sound, mostly women, made salaries similar to those of workers from K-mart or Target, with high-end salaries at eight dollars an hour.

The distinction in wages and titles among female employees created barriers between the two groups. Both cashiers and merchandise clerks rarely discussed interacting with each other at work, yet merchandise clerks used cashiers as a reference group for the perceived unfairness in pay and mobility. For instance, several clerks said they resented cashiers because they were doing the same job but getting paid differently. One white housewares clerk said, "Cashiers make twice what I do even though we both work the same hours" (12). These clerks often made themselves feel better by boasting about their freedom of movement around the store. However, merchandise clerks mainly discussed how they eventually wanted to "move up" into a cashier position so they could make more money.

The one status the women in my sample shared concerned their family responsibilities. Out of the eighteen women I spoke with at BGS, only four had children under eighteen years of age at home. The majority, 44 percent, had no children, and the remaining 33 percent had children over the age of eighteen. However, a large division did exist between married men with families and the rest of the employees. Men with small children were more likely than even women with children under eighteen to say they did little socializing with people outside of the workplace. This was mainly because the men were married (while the women with children tended to be divorced) and because they were older than most of the other workers.[3]

Even though cashiers and stockers made similar wages, stockers were in a better position to climb the corporate ladder. In order to become a salaried manager anywhere in the store, workers were mostly groomed as stockers. Cashiers' and stockers' variable access to job mobility, then, created distinctions among them even though their wages did not.

While on the job, workers joked and socialized with people nearby. This was harder for cashiers since they were stationed in one position. However, even they managed to converse with their fellow cashiers while working. The physical freedom that merchandise clerks, stockers, courtesy clerks and bakers enjoyed gave them more opportunity to discuss with their co-workers what tasks needed to be completed, to talk about family, and to complain about management. Indeed, complaining about management was central to the interactions that workers from different departments had with each other. Cross-position interactions took place mainly in two locations, the snack bar and the break room. One cashier said:

> When I'm on break, I like talking to people from other departments. Especially dairy, there are a lot of good people in that department. I know because my son is there. But seems like all we do lately is gripe about the front office.[4] (7)

Thus, what tied people together at BGS was their shared frustration with management.

Employees stated that they were most likely to interact with people socially outside of work when they shared the same job title. Seventy-six percent of the employees I interviewed said that they had monthly contact with at least one other person outside of work, and these interactions tended to be among people with the same job title, regardless of gender[5] and wages. For instance, one male cashier said, "Sometimes me, Suzie and Angela go to the bars. I asked Suz out once, but it didn't work out" (7). Strong social ties, in which workers had weekly contact with at least one person from the store, tended to be more gender homogeneous. Two cashiers, for instance, said they lived with fellow cashiers. On occasion, an employee from the store would throw a party, and these were the rare instances in which employees socialized together regardless of position, wage, or gender.

Workers at BGS agreed that, despite tension with upper management, the atmosphere at the workplace was pleasant. Workers, even across positions, were at least cordial with each other. When workers felt they were treated unfairly, they blamed either the organization or abstract and uncontrollable economic forces rather than co-workers. For instance, five women talked about feeling discriminated against because of their sex. However, each attributed the discrimination to something outside the company's control. One white cashier who complained about sexism at length said:

> I've got my disagreements with my . . . with the company. A lot of it's about sexism. But I know they have to meet a profit margin, bottom line. I know businesses are like that. I just wish they weren't. (14)

Thus, even if women saw men moving more rapidly into management positions, they did not blame their co-workers for their quick mobility.

Similarities and Differences at Geofelt Manufacturing

Geofelt was the first industry to locate in Pineville,[6] and besides the two hotels off the highway, it was the largest employer in town. The company was located on the edge of Pineville, about four miles down a road near the highway. Workers had no need to travel into the heart of town[7] nor through its neighborhoods. Like many small towns, Pineville seemed wary of outsiders;[8] the location of GM near the interstate did not seem accidental.

Only three people I interviewed lived in Pineville; the rest traveled, on average, thirty minutes each way to GM. Since many industries that settled in Alabama were scattered among small towns, commuting to work was not uncommon for workers. Indeed, seventeen out of the twenty workers had commuted to work before their job at GM. Most of the employees had heard about GM through a state-run program that trains and places residents into employment positions; three people had heard of the company from friends or relatives. While the five-dollar-an-hour starting wage was average in comparison with other companies in the area, the full health-coverage benefits for workers and their families made GM stand apart from other companies. Since most employees did not live in Pineville and had other job opportunities available, the workforce was not faced with complete dependency on GM for its survival.

Seventy-five percent of the workers I interviewed were married and ninety percent had children. However, having children did not stop some of the younger workers from going out after work and "partying" with friends. Of the four employees who said they had at least weekly contact with co-workers outside of work, three of them were younger than twenty-five and married with children. For instance, one young, white worker said that he went hunting and fishing with some of the other white workers on his shift during the season. Another young man, an African-American, said that during the summer prior to my interviews he and two African-American males from the same work team made weekly, and sometimes daily, visits to the river to drink beer and "hang out."[9] He said:

> When we worked days, towards the end of summer, it was bad, 'cause we'd meet down from the plant and we almost became alcoholics. Just drinking beers a few hours and go home. And we enjoyed it because we got to get some of our gripes out and just shoot the bull that we might not have got to do during the day. 'Cause when you're working all the time and on the go you don't really get to know the person much and so, we'd get together and have fun. (3)

Friendships in which people had weekly contact with co-workers were often limited by race, shift, and position. Employees stated that it was very difficult to socialize with workers on different shifts or positions because their schedules were so varied. For this reason, being transferred to a different shift/position was hard on workers with established social ties. The African-American worker who used to drink with his buddies during the summer said:

> I'm on a different shift now 'cause of the union, so I don't really know anybody. And there are so many new guys I need to make friends. And with the other guys, it's hard because some of us work late, some don't and then we live so far apart.

Seventy-five percent of GM workers said that they saw each other socially outside of work only once or twice a month. As at BGS, these interactions were the ones more likely to cross racial and shift lines; however, the majority stayed within race and shift. The content of these interactions varied by age. Younger workers, despite age and marital status, said they sometimes saw their co-workers at the hotel bar near the interstate at the GM exit. Older workers (over twenty-five) claimed their social ties had more to do with families, and these were the interactions most likely to cross race and shift lines.[10] For instance, one white man said:

> My best friend at work is Tommie [an African-American man]. I guess because our age is so close together we have a lot to relate to. We are both church-going people, and we go to the same denomination of church so we have a lot in common. So sometimes after church, we'll get our families together. (4)

Inside the company, workers were socially divided by position and, within positions, by shift. While there was a break room in the plant, warehouse people often ate with each other in the warehouse, while lab techs and the maintenance crew ate separately from each other and the forty-eight technicians. The techs complained that one of the reasons they needed a union was because they were not receiving any breaks, including for meals. This meant that their socializing was completed mainly on the job with people from their shift. After their shift, some workers socialized while baling waste together or getting ready to go home.

Even within the technicians' shifts, however, there was some division among workers based on the number of years they had worked for the company. The twelve employees with more than two years at the company were more jaded and skeptical about the plant; they remembered the harmony that had existed at the company's beginning. Younger workers felt more confident about the plant's future and their role within it. Furthermore, these younger workers did not complain as much about failing to get raises or yearly evaluations.

The division by years at the plant crossed racial lines. For example, half of the workers I interviewed brought up the issue of racial discrimination. Of these ten employees, six claimed that African-Americans were treated more harshly by supervisors and failed to get proper raises. All six employees had been with the company more than two years; four were African-American, two were white. Four of the workers who brought up racial discrimination during the interview were newer employees who said that, while they had heard racism was a problem at the plant, they had never witnessed it. Two of these four workers were African-American. One of them said:

> The people that got hired after me, they got treated pretty good. But before me, I would say most of the blacks out there they'd probably tell you that they feel discriminated against. I never experienced it so I can't say if they did or not.
> *Interviewer: So do you think that they were discriminated against?*
> I can't say if they did or didn't. I just never experienced it. (3)

All the workers who mentioned racial discrimination attributed the problem to management. No one mentioned problems with racism among workers themselves.

Despite the differences in perceptions about the plant, there was little animosity among workers and most of the technicians claimed they got along well with each other.[11] Employees did not see themselves as responsible for the problems at the plant. Rather, workers believed that the issues came from a middle management that ran amok. Once the president of the company became personally involved, employees believed, the company could turn itself around.

Summary

Homogeneity among workers helps invoke a sense of community and incites solidarity and, possibly, activism. Workers from BGS were separated from each other mostly by their positions and gender. The most likely time and place for mixed interactions were during people's breaks and lunches. However, on and off the job people socialized with co-workers much like themselves. Similarly at GM, workers were most likely to "hang out" with people outside of work when they shared the same position and race. Furthermore, technicians were further divided by shift and age group. At work, however, shift members, regardless of age and race, interacted with each other directly before and after work and, when possible, on the job. At both BGS and GM, then, the most important variable for defining sameness was people's job position (and shift). Interacting together gave people the opportunity to know each other and establish ties. Furthermore, gender at BGS and race at GM helped to establish friendships, with most close social ties between people of the same race or gender.

Workers' Ideologies and Aspirations[12]

The "American Dream," Chinoy suggests (1955), is a hegemonic tool that successfully keeps workers from collectively resisting capitalist control. Regardless of how hard workers toil, the survival of a capitalist economy depends on structural inequality. Only a small proportion of workers will be able to advance hierarchically. Yet the belief that hard work enables mobility, and the consequent aspirations towards advancement, keep employees from recognizing their common interests and mobilizing together (Halle 1984). In his study of blue-collar chemical workers, David Halle finds, "The better the chance of moving upward at work and the more secure their jobs, the more workers possess 'careers,' perhaps analogous to those of upper-white-collar managers and professionals, and the less likely they are to be conscious of class and to feel solidarity with each other" (149). Solidarity is hampered, then, the more workers align their interests with the company rather than each other and the more workers fail to question the structure of work.

I find that BGS workers grew less committed to the "American Dream" while GM workers still hoped that they could climb the job ladder within their company. Workers from BGS and GM, however, did have two characteristics in common. First, they both saw themselves as "rebellious," at least when it came to confronting management about their individual jobs. Second, they both believed that, while workers knew their specific jobs better than management, hierarchies in the workplace were necessary for the smooth functioning of companies.

Bob's Grocery Stores

Grocery stores commonly attract workers who are not attached to the job and see their employment as temporary. Indeed, the turnover rate for grocery workers is relatively high. In BGS's early years, however, a more committed worker was attracted to the "superstore." Employees at BGS felt devoted to the company since wages and benefits were better than at other grocery stores. Plus, workers could move up the corporate ladder without a college education. When the Canadian company transformed BGS into the image of its competition, workers said their commitment to the company decreased. Of the thirty people I interviewed, only thirteen said they were committed to their jobs. Four workers said they were working at BGS only until they completed their education and attained "real" jobs, and thirteen said they were no longer committed to a company that gave them little job security.[13] A twelve-year journeyman stocker had this to say about why he had gone back to school:

> Working at Bob's used to be an event. Saturdays at Bob's used to be an event, that's when we changed over from one ad to the next. We had all kinds of help; we had all kinds of business because we were pretty much the only show in town. You could get excited about it; you could get motivated, and it was a lot of fun. There was a sense of community in the store. But the company wasn't prepared for the competition when they came. They made so many changes and so many were done so unfairly that ah, people aren't staying. You see a lot of people are leaving the company. A lot of people are going to school right now. I could name six or seven in the same education program I'm in. It's just not any fun anymore. It's really a depressing place to work. (30)

Many workers also said that their commitment atrophied when they realized that there was no longer any job mobility. Of course, employees could become managers paid on an hourly basis. However, not one employee was envious of the amount of work for which managers were responsible and the disproportionately low wages they were paid. Indeed, the company was having problems filling managerial positions.

The hard work and low wages of managers reveal why twenty-seven out of the thirty workers I interviewed said they did not want to move up in the company.[14] One white stocker explained:

> The managers, I think, get a buck more an hour than we do and it really isn't much considering all the headaches they have to put with. They work way too many hours for the pay. I have a boss who the company is threatening to fire because he doesn't get enough work done. But there's no way we can get all the work done with the amount of people we got working here. So there he is working his buns off and his family life is hurting. He'll probably get divorced soon. They all do. (5)

The toll exacted for being a manager at BGS—long hours, low pay, and a disrupted family life—was a cost too steep for many employees.

Of the twenty-seven who said they did not wish to move up in the company, twenty-two admitted that, at one point, before the change in managerial responsibility, ascending the job ladder had been their goal. One cashier stated succinctly, "Of course I'd want to move up. Who wouldn't want to tell people what to do?" (6). It was not "dreams of mobility" that BGS workers shunned when they stated they had no desire to move up in the company, but the endless responsibilities that managers faced daily for few rewards.

While mobility for workers ceased and job commitment weakened, employees did not collectively protest the changes at BGS. Instead, workers tended to "speak out" individually. Indeed, 60 percent of the employees defined themselves as "troublemakers" or "rebels."[15] The following are some examples of how workers claimed they defended themselves against management:

> *White, Female Cashier:* I'm a little bit on the rebellious side. When I'm being screwed over, I don't take it. When they change something and it's take away time, I'm the first one to open my mouth in the store. (2)
>
> *White, Female Merchandise Clerk:* When my manager first came over I wasn't too impressed with him. They come over with a chip, and that's bad. He told me that I couldn't do things my way anymore but I had to do everything his way. I said, "Excuse me, do I not do the work?" And

he said, "Yes." And I said, "Do I not do more than what I'm supposed to here?" And he said, "Yes." And I said, "Your rules don't apply to me." And I walked away, saying, "You want to be boss, you be boss with somebody else. I'm doing my job, I don't want to hear a lecture. I come home I can hear that shit. I don't have to go to work and hear it [laugh]." I just told him and I've never had a problem with him. (12)

White, Male Stocker: I tend to be more outspoken than a lot of people, and I think if anyone else had a problem with the manger they'd probably never say anything. Whereas I'm much more upfront and I'd go right up to him and tell him. (16)

Workers were motivated to "speak up" when managers challenged the way they completed their jobs. Seventy percent of employees believed that workers, and especially themselves, knew better how to do their jobs than management. For instance, one white, female merchandise clerk admitted:

Well, I think employees know best how to do their jobs. They know what customers want and need. Management doesn't even deal with customers. So management should be listening to the employees, but they don't. (3)

Thus, employees believed that they could legitimately "rebel" against managerial decisions.

Even though workers claimed that they knew the inner workings of the store better than managers, they deeply believed that managers were still very necessary to the company. Curiously, the manager's role was seen as vital even if the manager did not do the job competently. One white cashier from BGS explained:

Sometimes I feel like a one-woman show. I mean when it's late at night and the manager is not up at the front and I need him. So I do his job too.
Interviewer: So do you think you need a manager then?
I don't know, well, yeah. Who would give us raises or make sure we get our evaluations? Who would have the authority to say, you're this or that? If we're all at the same level, then I wouldn't want anyone telling me what to do. (23)

The young woman expressed a common sentiment held among employees. Managers were important, not necessarily because they had more knowledge than the employees, but because they had more authority. Workers felt comfortable questioning the decisions supervisors made, but not the authority structure that gave them the power to make those decisions. Supervisors were interpreted as necessary because hierarchy was necessary. Repeating the words of the cashier above, "Who would give us raises?" Thus, even while the new owners halted job mobility, causing a decrease in workers' job commitment, BGS employees believed that the existence of hierarchy gave management the legitimacy to make any decisions it deemed necessary.

Geofelt Manufacturing

Most of the workers from GM came from labor-intensive jobs, such as construction and traditional textile. The move to a high-tech, capital-intensive industry gave many workers a sense of pride. One African-American technician said:

> The job, it's just very unique. To us down South, it's more of what I call a lazy man's job because it's just push-button. It's just basically run by computers and compressed air. You don't have to do much manual labor. That's what's so interesting about it. You would think this kind of job would be in a more metropolitan area. So there's a lot of job pride. (16)

"Job pride" was among the reasons workers gave for being committed to the company.[16] The benefits package and opportunity for job mobility also kept them attached to GM. Five of the employees said they were not committed either because GM was simply a job until they could become self-employed or because they did not see themselves as able to move up.

Seventy-five percent of GM workers did perceive job mobility as possible and desired the chance to move up.[17] The company was young and thriving and, workers reasoned, would need experienced people to competently handle its inevitable expansion. Employees gave two reasons why they wanted the chance to ascend the hierarchy. First, workers desired higher wages, more authority and more flexibility; they perceived that moving up would provide them with these rewards. Second, a few workers suggested that the supervisor's job was a sinecure and that they would like to be able to receive wages for doing nothing. One veteran African-American technician said:

> I would like to be a supervisor because they don't do nothing. They have two guys under them to take care of the lines, so therefore, they don't really have to do nothing. They just sit in the office all day long. If I have a problem, too bad. I call and they come down and assist me for a few minutes and that's it. (1)

Many workers agreed that supervisors labored very little. However, they felt this was a problem with the individual supervisors at GM rather than a problem endemic to the position. Thus, workers reasoned that if they were supervisors, or even higher, they would certainly do a more competent job. First, they would be nice and respectful to workers. As one African-American technician put it:

> A good manager needs to be a people's person. The workplace should please the employee because he's the one that's making the money. He's the one that's the backbone of the company. I think that management should take a stance and say we respect the employee; he's the most important resource that we have, and we should do everything to make him comfortable. I think management, they think that you have to be uncomfortable, that they have to put you in a position where you have to feel tense and tight all the time and you can't do your job. I think that is the worst way to manage the company and so I would do a much better job. (15)

Employees would also do a more efficient job because they would include workers more in the decision-making at the plant. Given that supervisors were not even doing the job, worker input was seen as imperative for completing the job well. These technicians explain:

> *African-American Technician:* I say to myself all the time, some of these guys have been here since the place opened and they should have more input. And some of the newer guys, we wonder why the older guys don't say anything, but it's probably because no one will listen to them. I mean, we know what's going on, we know how to make this place run better, but they don't ask us, they don't think we know anything and that's the first thing I'd change if I became supervisor. (7)

> *White Technician:* As a supervisor you need to realize that workers know what they're doing and are trying to do the best they can. You need to get some more input from other technicians on how to correct problems and get things done. 'Cause they're the ones working, you know. (10)

Workers concurred that the company was unnecessarily lowering productivity by ignoring employee input and that, if they became people with authority, the company would abandon this faulty business strategy.

Even though a majority of GM employees desired a higher position, 55 percent of the workers I interviewed said they were not afraid to voice their opinion to managers, at least when they, themselves, were being harmed.[18] Indeed, most workers believed that they were unique in their willingness to confront managers. As this white technician stated:

> I don't bow down to my bosses. I tell them exactly how it is. I'm very expressive when it comes to releasing stress, especially to somebody that

pushed me. My managers don't appreciate that. They want someone who's a yes-man and they get it. (5)

Workers said that they were willing to confront managers when they made "wrong" decisions, when managers were being discriminatory or unfair towards them, and when they were just being "stupid." However, even though workers claimed they challenged management individually, they did nothing collectively until the organizing campaign.

GM employees complained about managers and felt they were many times incompetent, but 87 percent still believed that managers were necessary. Clearly, workers knew more about their particular job but, like BGS workers, GM employees felt managers were important because hierarchy was important. As these GM technicians expressed it:

> *White Technician:* The technician knows how to do the job the best because the supervisor loses touch. He's bound with too much paperwork to know what's going on the line. Sometimes you wonder, why don't we do so and so, but we do it the supervisor's way.
>
> *Interviewer: Who should be making those decisions?*
> I think ultimately it should fall on the supervisor. That's why he's in that position. You need a leader somewhere. (13)
>
> *African-American Technician:* Oh, yes. I think management is really important. I believe that! I'm not saying that a company shouldn't have managers. I'm saying that somebody needs to be in charge, somebody needs to be there to make decisions and to implement them. (15)

For employees, the decision-making hierarchy was viewed as a natural and necessary part of the enterprise, even if it did include the fundamental contradiction that managers were less competent than workers about making decisions regarding workers' jobs.

However, GM employees felt that the upper echelon had one advantage that made them indispensable: managers had more information about the workings of the entire plant. I asked one African-American warehouse man why managers were necessary given that they did very little. He said:

> Well, they know about the materials, how it's supposed to be sold, they know about other things, goings-on with other departments, they just know more. And they are there if the customer complains, but as far as loading a truck the right way, they don't know. (9)

Since the supervisor's position enabled him to have more knowledge about the whole plant's operation, workers perceived that his authority over them was justified.

Summary

The layoffs and high work demands at BGS created a jaded workforce with waning commitment towards the company. Most employees did not want to move ahead, which perhaps explains why 60 percent claimed they were willing to question managerial decisions concerning their jobs. While BGS workers desired the "American Dream," most did not believe they could attain mobility from the company any longer. Workers at GM, however, were more optimistic about their future in the company. Most employees desired to move up, mainly because they felt they could do a better job than their supervisor, but also because they wanted more material rewards. Wanting a higher position did not stop 55 percent of GM workers from speaking up for themselves against management. Like BGS employees, GM workers felt they knew better how to do their own jobs and felt justified in voicing their opinions. Both BGS and GM employees, however, believed that the work hierarchy was an inevitable and necessary part of the workplace.

Conclusion

As workers share similar life experiences, they are likely to perceive their interests similarly and to act in concert to protect those interests. Traditionally, cohesion is thought to emerge under certain conditions within the labor process and work organization, when people's demographic characteristics are the same and when employees hold similar workplace ideologies. An ideal research situation would enable me to compare the organizing campaigns of two workgroups within the same industry and with comparable gender and race compositions. However, the state of labor organizing at present, in which it is difficult to win an election much less attain a contract within a reasonable time, forces me to work with the opportunities I have. Thus, I cannot determine definitively how industry, gender and race affected activism before the organizing campaigns.

I can provide narrative descriptions of workers' situations and their perceptions of their situations. Furthermore, I can compare how active men and women at BGS and whites and African-Americans at GM were before, during, and after the campaigns, and to what workers themselves attributed their activism. All of this provides persuasive evidence that worker activism (as I describe it in the next chapter) was influenced by something other than the fact that the two workgroups shared different workplace and worker characteristics.

In this chapter, I have shown that the greatest similarities between BGS and GM workers were that (1) they both faced similar levels of "intensive interaction" and increased emotional "distance" with managers, (2) they both tended to be socially divided within the stores based on job position, gender, and race, and (3) they both believed hierarchy was a necessary, functional aspect of the workplace. The greatest difference between BGS and GM workers was that BGS workers had fewer expectations that they could attain the "American Dream" at their workplace. Most importantly, however, workers from both BGS and GM before the organizing campaigns tended to resist the increased changes at the companies individually rather than collectively. In the next chapter I discuss how the structure of organizing campaigns is theoretically and empirically related to the creation of collective resistance.

4

The Organizing Campaigns at Bob's Grocery Stores and Geofelt Manufacturing

Introduction

Carole Pateman's fundamental assertion in *Participation and Democratic Theory* (1970) is that institutional arrangements explain activism among citizens better than individual predispositions. In *Cultures of Solidarity* (1988), Fantasia asserts a similar argument in his conceptualization of class consciousness as more process than dichotomy; it is something that emerges among employees through their interactions. Under this conception of "class consciousness," cohesion is not a characteristic of a person or place, but develops within social situations between workers. Fantasia states, "[A]nalyses of class consciousness should be based on actions, organizational capabilities, institutional arrangements, and the values that arise within them, rather than on attitudes abstracted from the context of social action" (11). Finally, Goffman further claims that social context is imperative for understanding individual behavior. He contends that organizational structures generate meaning for their participants and, subsequently, shape individuals' reactions to organizations (1974).

The focus of this chapter, then, is simply to describe the organizing campaigns in which workers participated. I must understand the contexts within which these two workgroups organized before I explain how workers from Bob's Grocery Stores (BGS) and Geofelt Manufacturing (GM) responded to the campaigns.

The Comprehensive Campaign at Bob's Grocery Stores

Bob's Grocery Stores is one of eight chains in the metropolitan area surrounding Phoenix, Arizona. The grocery workers' union successfully organized three of the eight chains by the time the BGS campaign started. A fourth chain was organized during the twenty-month BGS campaign. The statewide organization of these chains made the grocery union the largest union in Arizona, representing almost twenty thousand workers. In the eighties, the grocery union expanded to cover employees from companies besides food stores. However, the bulk of its membership still consisted of workers from the grocery industry.

The union campaign at BGS began in March 1991. Even though the union had been getting weekly calls from disgruntled BGS employees for years before the campaign began, the union decided to wait until it had the resources to be effective. The grocery workers' union had long targeted BGS for an organizing campaign because one-tenth of the workforce, the meat employees, were already represented by the union. The meat department had been organized twenty years before when the International Butchers' Union and the American Retailers' Union were still separate entities. When the two unions merged in 1980, all supermarkets with only part of the workforce represented by the labor union became obvious targets for organizing efforts. One organizer described the instrumental necessity of organizing the entire store: "We knew that in order to get the meat contracts at BGS up to the level of the industry, not the substandard that they've had for years, we needed to have the leverage of the rest of the workers organized" (4). Organizing the retail side of BGS would not only give the union leverage with the meat contract, but also strength in the grocery industry by making five out of the eight grocery chains union.

The campaign began with a massive sign-up in which forty-five organizers, many of them paid "volunteers" from other grocery chains, went to BGS to collect authorization card signatures from employees. At least 30 percent of the workforce must sign authorization cards before a union election can take place. However, this organizing campaign differed from traditional campaigns in that the union wanted to use employees' signatures to convince the company to recognize the union, not to establish an election. The organizers had two advantages in pursuing their goal of gathering cards. First, BGS allowed organizers access to the stores. While they could not "solicit" employees on the job, they could station themselves comfortably in the snack bar and talk to employees on their breaks. Being present to employees at the workplace gave organizers considerable opportunity to establish trust and rapport with the workers. Second, with the meat department already union, organizers were contractually entitled access to the back of the store. As long as organizers did not disrupt the ability of workers to perform their jobs, they were permitted to talk with the employees in the meat department, including grocery workers who walked back to the meat area to talk to a friend or complete a work task. Organizers, ostensibly, were not allowed anywhere in the store except the snack bar and the meat department. Of course, in order to get from one point to the other, they had to stroll the distance. In reality, this gave them total access to the stores. Organizers used these "strolls" to look for employees they knew still had not signed authorization cards. For instance, they might spot a stocker building a display case and nonchalantly begin a conversation unrelated to unions, say about fast-moving items. At the close of the discourse the organizer would encourage the employee to stop by the snack bar and sign a union card. If caught in the aisle talking with an employee, the organizers would simply tell the manager that they were just passing through on the way to the meat department or asking about an item to purchase.

The initial sign-up lasted four and a half months, from the middle of March until the beginning of August, and was described as successful by the union. One organizer said:

> The initial sign-up was just a probe, to see what kind of response we would get. There were hundreds of people lined up to sign cards the first week. We signed hundreds and hundreds of cards. So, clearly, they were waiting for us. (4)

Store modifications that the new owners were making sparked employees' interest in the union. The original owner of the chain, Bob Smith, had sold his company seven years before the campaign. With his departure, as discussed earlier, many changes occurred in the company that left workers angry and dissatisfied. Bob Smith had run the company paternalistically, creating an atmosphere of familial intimacy. One organizer admitted, "We could never have organized this store when Bob Smith was here. Everybody was very loyal to him" (4). A Latina cashier who had worked for the company during Bob's tenure said, "They were like a second family. So I really enjoyed working for them, that's why I kept going back each time I left to take care of my family'' (13). Even though Bob was, at times, inflexible in his demands, including making employees work off the clock, he was very personable. When the Canadian company bought Bob's, Smith's paternalism was replaced with impersonal bureaucracy. The new owners and managers at the top of the hierarchy distanced themselves from those at the bottom, which created a sense of alienation among employees. The company also reduced an entire level of middle managers, cut the hours of long-term employees, and hired new employees at lower wages. The reorganization harmed morale. Employees who at one point had been willing to put in extra hours for free admitted that they were now only putting in the time for which they were scheduled, whether or not the job was completed.

Of the thirty employees I interviewed, 76 percent claimed that a union was necessary at their workplace, citing impersonal managerial relations, layoffs, and reduced hours to justify it. A white, male scanning coordinator explained:

> The first layoff cut [almost] all middle managers. We went from seven to ten managers in every store to three. I thought that was sad because those were the people who know the business. The part-timers that they hired didn't know anything. Shortly after, they made all full-timers, part-timers. They wanted to run the whole store with part-timers for the sake of flexibility. They said that in our business they need flexibility. So now we're all working twice as hard, doing managers' jobs, and not getting paid for it. So one thing led to another, the union came in and said, ''Hey, this isn't how it is supposed to be. We'll fix it.'' And that's how the union came about. (1)

Before the union could ''fix'' the problem, however, the workplace had to be unionized. Organizers were convinced that a successful union campaign at BGS was feasible given the number of employees who signed authorization cards. Yet before embarking upon a full-fledged Comprehensive Campaign, the union local president took the gathered signatures and asked the company for recognition. As expected, BGS did not grant the union the authority to be the official representative of the workforce. Hence, the Comprehensive Campaign materialized.

At this time, organizers left the stores and union officials from the regional office in California were called upon to determine how the strategy of the Comprehensive Campaign should develop. All of the decision-making about the campaign came from the regional office.

The organizers simply were given assignments and told to fulfill them. The officials in control decided that all resources should be focused on gathering data about the company and that information would be collected by several of the local union representatives. Representatives collected data of two types: first, financial information (who owned the company, what the company's assets were, who the investors in the company were, where the company invested its money), and second, labor violation information (did employees have EEOC—Equal Employment Opportunity Commission—complaints, were wage and hour and child labor laws being breached, were health regulations being violated). Since the union had access to the meat department, details collected about labor violations came mainly from this source. For instance, organizers documented health violations by using a hidden camera to film common illegal procedures that workers were encouraged to practice. Less frequently and less systematically, union representatives also asked retail workers whether they were denied raises because of their sex or race or if they were scheduled to work hours they were not supposed to, given that they were still underage.

The union only allowed ten BGS employees from the twenty-four-store chain to become involved in the union campaign. Two of these workers came from the meat department and were already union members. Because the union wanted to maintain control over who had access to information, organizers felt justified in being selective in whom they permitted to become active in the Comprehensive Campaign. One chosen worker said, "This one guy, he was sure mad that he wasn't allowed to be on the original organizing committee. But he was at the victory celebration anyway." Active employees spent time at work talking with co-workers about the union and time after work helping to create and pass out fliers. They also participated in media activities, such as appearing on local cable stations to discuss why forming a union at BGS was necessary. Unlike the majority of BGS employees, they were given the same information about the campaign process as the paid union organizers. This information, however, was often limited to the types of tasks that they were assigned to complete by the regional officials.

Organizers admitted to me that secrecy was needed to keep the management at BGS unaware of the union's strategy. "Of course there were secrets," one active BGS employee said, "because it's a war and there's a campaign going on. There's a lot of secret strategy involved in winning'' (5). The union reasoned that the information it collected gave it maximum leverage if the company had no idea that data were being gathered. This meant that excluding the workforce from the union's strategy was an essential component of the union's Comprehensive Campaign. Withholding secrets extended to the organizers of the campaign as well. Organizers, of course, knew that information was being accumulated. Yet they were not informed when the company would be asked for recognition or even which information they collected would be used to bargain with the company. One of the persons in charge of the campaign stated, ''Sometimes it's best not to show any of your cards, even to your good friends'' (6). Worker participation in the campaign, then, was kept to a minimum so that the union could more effectively gather and use information.

The majority of employees at BGS had no idea that union representatives were collecting information to aid in organizing efforts. Indeed, when the organizers disappeared from the stores after the initial sign-up, workers assumed that the campaign had fallen through. A white, female cashier said:

> They came in and we were all so excited. Then all of a sudden, they disappeared. It was so quick that we thought they abandoned us. Really, we didn't know what to think. (2)

Organizers disappeared from the stores as part of the ''secretive'' strategy of collecting information about BGS. They also withdrew because of a new commitment by the union to organize another grocery chain, Taylor's. Taylor's had recently expanded to Arizona from California, where it was a union store. The regional office decided that the Arizona local should focus its energies momentarily on Taylor's, a campaign it perceived as simple given the store's historical relationship with the union. Organizers, then, were sent to Taylor's to collect workers' signatures. As predicted, after collecting the signatures of a majority of the employees, the grocery union was recognized by Taylor's management as the official bargaining agent for the workforce. Several of the organizers I informally spoke with voiced discomfort at the sudden change in the union's focus. ''I don't know how smart it was to completely pull out of Bob's,'' one organizer admitted. ''It made the campaign drag on and many of the workers assumed we abandoned them'' (2). Including the time to negotiate a contract, the union was away from the BGS campaign for six months.

Yet once the Taylor's contract was signed, the union refocused its energy on BGS.

After the end of the Taylor's campaign, five international organizers were brought from the D.C. office to work on the BGS Comprehensive Campaign. These "specialized" organizers are paid to travel across the United States to help in campaigns that the international office defines as significant. The supervisor of the specialized team and the head of the regional office shared decision-making power during the BGS campaign. The international organizers worked in concert with five organizers from the regional office and eleven local union representatives. Together, the organizers gathered information, occasionally went to the stores to talk to workers, and intermittently made house calls to employees. After the successful Taylor's campaign, organizers again went inside the stores for a massive employee sign-up. Although organizers once again collected signatures from a majority of the workers, the campaign still developed slowly for two reasons: first, the international, regional and local organizers had other commitments they were working on besides the BGS campaign, and second, the company chose to pay the fines for the health and safety violations the organizers exposed rather than concede to the union.

Finally, in November 1991, an active BGS employee nonchalantly described to the international supervisor an unusual situation that had occurred at his store. A woman, not associated with the union, was handing out protest fliers to co-workers about having to work Christmas day. The activist described how the campaign leader reacted:

> Fred closed the book he was working in and said, "Stop right there." He said, "Tell me about this Christmas thing." So I told him. He said, "I want the details. Do you know this girl? Do you know what department she works in? Where can we find her? Can she help us?" He said, "Here's a situation where we are now behind the wave. That's not good. We need to get out in front of the wave."

The campaign leader frankly admitted to the activist that the union needed to "control" the issues that defined the campaign, and "this Christmas thing" was obviously an issue. The union, then, exposed publicly the BGS policy of requiring employees to work on Christmas to garner favorable media attention. The union solicited support from the religious community and sided with a prominent Catholic priest who asked customers not to shop at BGS on Christmas Day. The local news stations broadcasted the Christmas dilemma eight times in the month of December, interviewing two union activists about the injustice of having to spend the day away from their families. The store remained open, however, despite the extensive media attention.[1]

Besides the local news media, the union also used cable stations to broadcast violations experienced by BGS employees. The lead international organizer discussed on television child labor violations, wage and hour violations, and the cutting of full-time employees to part-time. These tactics created community support for the union's drive to organize at BGS. Since grocery stores were abundant in Phoenix, consumers could easily avoid grocery shopping at BGS. This made the broadcasts a potentially effective strategy for encouraging management to negotiate. The union claimed that the media attention did harm company sales. However, company profits had been on a downward slope before this period, which was why BGS decided to remain open on Christmas Day.

Of the thirty workers I spoke with, ten were aware of the media attention focused on BGS. Rather than appreciating the union's attempts to portray the company in a negative light, however, eight of the ten workers felt uncomfortable with the union's approach. Employees claimed, first and foremost, that the outsider status of the union gave it "no right" to discuss BGS. The scanning coordinator I spoke with said:

> We separated ourselves from the organizers who were outside, picketing stores, getting arrested. How did they know what's going on? They didn't even work here. (1)

Second, workers felt that they were implicated in some of the wage and hour and child labor law violations mentioned by the media. A white, male stocker who eventually became shop steward in the union said:

> Sometimes I thought they [the union] played a little dirty pool because they would call OSHA and say, "Hey, there are all these violations, come out and we'll put it in the paper." Those safety violations were so small. But they did it for publicity. And I'll tell you what, it was not in the best interest of the employee. With that kind of tactic, they couldn't give a shit about us. That's my opinion. (30)

Finally, employees were concerned that, if the consumer boycott was successful, the workers, rather than the company, would be harmed.

Workers believed that they would be fired before managers allowed themselves to be hurt financially.

The campaign finale occurred in October and November 1992. After collecting information and talking to BGS employees, all the international, regional and local players in the organizing process gathered in Phoenix to engage in another employee sign-up. Directed by a regional official, forty organizers were sent to the stores to collect signatures. For six weeks, organizers were located inside BGS stores talking to employees and getting union authorization cards signed. There were two organizers per store, with ninety to 120 workers per store. Union officials told organizers that their main goal should be to collect as many signed cards as possible. Toward this end, organizers met every morning in a classroom-style room where the campaign supervisor stood at the head. The organizers had to call out the number of cards they had acquired the day before. Organizers with high numbers were given standing ovations. Organizers who collected only a few cards were asked for an explanation and told to do better that day.

Union representatives said that the meetings fostered a competitive environment among organizers. Three organizers admitted to me that they sometimes "padded" their cards, meaning that they asked workers who had already signed union cards to sign another. Some organizers also acknowledged that at times they distorted the truth in order to convince workers to sign a card. For instance, organizers would tell employees that signing a card only meant that the employee wanted a union election held[2] or that workers who signed cards would receive a monetary bonus when the union became the bargaining agent for BGS.

The most common approach organizers employed in the card quest, however, was to appeal to workers' sense of practicality. Workers were informed of the instrumental aspects of having a union at the workplace. A union, workers were told, was an organization that provided employees with job security, nice benefit packages, and high wages. The employees' role in the union was simple: all they needed to do was pay a small portion of their paychecks each week so that union representatives could be placed in the stores and ensure that the company played by the rules laid out in the contract. Here are some examples of how workers described their interactions with organizers:

White, Union Cashier: So I basically talked to these guys from out of state and they told me how they were going to improve conditions, how I would have job security, how my pension would roll over up . . . what else did they tell me? Basically that was it. (6)

Latina, Union Cashier: When you went on break, people would approach you. They would show you booklets and explain how they could help us keep our jobs. And then they give you cards, you sign them and that's about it. (17)

White, Nonunion Stocker: The first campaign, the work issue they basically screamed about was job security. They could prevent you from being laid off. Second campaign they came in with benefits and said they could save your job. They basically tried to sell the same thing both times. (10)

Once the employee was "sold" and signed a card, the interaction between worker and organizer was complete.

Sometimes, in an attempt to procure more signatures, organizers solicited help from BGS employees. First, to find out who worked at the store, organizers asked some workers to get them the discarded time schedules, which contained employees' names, phone numbers, and addresses. Second, some workers were given extra cards and asked to sign up friends. For employees who volunteered, these small requests were worth their time if the union really could make things better at the workplace. The most active worker with whom I spoke was a Latina woman who obtained an employee list for the organizers and convinced her friends to sign union cards. She said, "I didn't regret getting things for them because I was trying to help them out so that they could help us out." (16)

The only attempt organizers made to create solidarity among workers was the dissemination of a publication called "The Snackbar Snooper." The ten active BGS employees helped to write articles and interview friends about the worsening conditions at the chain and the need for a union. Unfortunately, most employees were not aware that their co-workers helped to write the newsletter. Instead, they believed that the organizers, who were perceived as outsiders, penned the defaming articles about BGS. Thus, workers did not take the newsletter seriously.

Union supervisors rotated organizers from store to store, also a strategy to collect more signatures. Organizers had an easier time "strolling" through the stores talking to employees when managers did not know who they were. Because workers were also unaware of the organizers' identity from one day to the next, this strategy also kept the organizers from establishing ties with employees. One organizer stated, "I understand completely why they wanted us to keep moving through the stores, but it made it real hard to get some workers to trust us." (2)

All in all, the union's strategies allowed it to attain the signatures of 65 percent of the workers. To the surprise of most BGS workers, management finally agreed in November to let the union represent BGS. Workers found out about management's decision through a letter posted on the time clock in each store. A white cashier described what happened:

> The campaign was real aggressive in the beginning, and it really quieted down for like a year and then all of a sudden we got a letter from the main office that said if we wanted the union, we could have it. We're still trying to figure out what happened all of a sudden to change management like that. (6)

All workers expressed similar astonishment that the "antiunion" company finally accepted the union.

The Blitz at Geofelt Manufacturing

The clothing workers' union campaign at GM began when a discontented employee phoned the union district office located forty miles from the company. Unlike the ripe situation at BGS, however, in which part of the workforce and half of the industry in town were already union, there was little impetus for the union to engage in an organizing campaign at GM. The workplace numbered only seventy eligible employees. Moreover, there was no other industry within a thirty-mile radius, much less other unionized geotextile plants. The small size of the plant made organizers think seriously before embarking upon a potentially expensive organizing campaign. One organizer admitted:

> Geofelt is a campaign we would not typically conduct. It only has seventy workers. In a perfect world, size wouldn't matter. We could organize anyone who wanted to be in a union. In reality, it takes tremendous resources and time to organize and in many cases the larger size allows you the resources that you need to win and secure a first contract. Unions are not rich organizations. We operate on our members' dues so we have to look practically. With Geofelt, a plant with seventy people, we will not benefit from their dues, considering the time we will spend in the plant with the workers. (3)

Despite the size limitation, a regional office representative from At-
lanta met personally with the employee from GM who originally contacted the union. Simultaneously, the targeting office gathered information about GM. The union had two goals before beginning a
campaign. First, they wanted to learn more about the workers. What
were their complaints? Did dissatisfaction spread beyond the person
who called? If so, how many workers were upset? Second, they also
desired information about the company. Who owned the company?
What was the financial state of the company?[3] Did it have other
plants? If so, were they union?

The union investigation revealed that GM was owned by a parent
company in Austria, which expanded beyond its national borders
when it developed the GM plant in Alabama. The parent company
was well known in its home country and financially lucrative. The
union uncovered one piece of crucial information during its research:
the parent company was itself unionized. Hence, the company, at best,
was not resistant to unions and, at least, could not feign ignorance
about the process of unionization. The information, along with con-
firmation that disappointment within the company ran beyond the original caller, convinced the union that an organizing campaign could be
won with relatively little time and resources.

The Blitz began in February 1993. The "disgruntled" employee
who originally phoned the union supplied the organizers with a phone
and address list of all line workers and shipping clerks, the majority
of the workforce. The list of employees was imperative for the Blitz
campaign. The object of the Blitz is to speak to as many workers as
possible in a condensed time period before the employer even learns
that a union campaign has begun. The company thus has no time to
mount effective scare tactics. Since union organizers did not have
access to the GM plant and needed to maintain a secret presence, the
worker address list allowed organizers to discreetly visit employees'
homes.

The home visits to GM employees were done within the customary
three-day period by volunteer organizers from the union in nearby
districts and by two paid organizers from the regional office. Upon
arriving at the employees' homes, the organizers introduced themselves and asked to speak with the workers about the union. Most of
the GM employees were curious about the union and were willing to
hear what the organizers had to say.

Organizers informed workers during these visits that only a union, through its generation of employee unity, could create the necessary changes in the workplace. One young, white technician described his first contact with a volunteer organizer:

> At the time I was living about forty-five minutes away and someone from Crenshaw's [a union plant] came out there. I had to tell them that I didn't know how I felt about the union. I told them I was willing to listen to them, though, and they understood. What I kind of liked about it was they didn't try to pressure me into anything. They let me do what I was going to do and let me make up my own mind. 'Cause I hate that. So a man that's in the union from Crenshaw's come by and showed me what his contract looked like, what they had got and stuff. And he said that we'd need to stick together to get this thing done. That guy from Crenshaw, that helped me a lot to be able to talk to someone else represented by the same group. It let me know that you can get a good contract and they will work with the workers, the people they are representing, rather than just try to do it all for them. I wouldn't like that at all, if they just came in and did everything and you had no say. That's when I decided to go to sign a card and go to a meeting. (10)

During these visits, organizers explained that getting union cards signed was only the first step in organizing the workplace. A six-week election period would follow in which it was imperative for employees to come together and vote the union in. Organizers also asked interested workers if they knew of fellow employees who would like to sign a union card. This tactic provided them with some names that were not on their address list and gave them insight into which employees they should be visiting. After the three-day canvassing of GM employees, the union had the requisite 30 percent employee signatures to file a campaign election with the NLRB.

While organizers were successful at attaining signatures, they were not quite as effective at keeping the emergent organizing campaign secret from the company. Employees of GM began murmuring about the possibility of a union. Somehow this hushed talk found its way to the management's attention. There were rumors among workers about how GM management found out about the campaign. One worker claimed that, while he was in the washroom speaking to a fellow prounion employee, a company "stooge," hiding in the toilet stall, eavesdropped on their conversation and reported immediately to management. Another worker claimed that he accidentally revealed the organizing plan by conversing with a co-worker who turned out to be against unionizing. The breach of secrecy was not harmful, however.

It simply meant that when two GM employees approached management to ask for union recognition, management was already prepared with a "No" answer.[4] The union expected GM to deny them recognition as the official bargaining agent. Unlike the grocery workers' union at BGS, however, organizers did not proceed by launching into a Comprehensive Campaign. Rather, they filed the necessary signatures with the NLRB and began a worker-intensive organizing campaign. The election date was set for the middle of March, the conventional six-week period it takes for the NLRB to collect and process necessary information.

Many GM workers were excited about the chance to unionize and reestablish positive work relations. Similar to the situation at BGS, in which workers did not feel a union was necessary until middle managers were fired and full-time employees were losing their benefits, the changing work situation at GM made employees feel that a union was required. One white technician, who had been with the company for six years, described the change:

> When I first hired in, it was a smaller company. Everybody knew everybody. They had a lot of activities and functions, and it was more on the basis of once you hired in you become a part of a family. When they had just one line, they preached good quality. Well, when they fired the new line up, they put quantity over quality. I think the difference is in the management. (19)

Workers felt that, when the company first opened, they were able to discuss with managers how to make the system function better, and managers not only listened, but also instituted some of the ideas. Unfortunately, this camaraderie was challenged when a new plant manager was hired approximately three years before the organizing campaign. Supervisors, with the permission and perhaps prompting of the new manager, did not listen to the ideas of workers any longer. Workers also expressed a growing awareness of racial discrimination. The new manager was white, as were all other managers. Yet, according to both black and white workers, he alone was openly racist, often using prejudiced language, and did not see that as a conflict in his role as manager. His racism also affected workers' wages. Black workers were not evaluated for raises as often as white workers. Furthermore, when evaluations did occur, black employees often were not evaluated as highly as their white co-workers. One white worker revealed:

> From the time the plant opened until just recently, there was no black supervisor or black upper management whatsoever, which was a bone of contention with the black people. They were slower to get raises. They were put upon more under certain circumstances; more was expected of them than a white person. (5)

Employees of GM believed that the deteriorating relationship between management and workers stemmed from the bad attitude of the new plant manager and was not a structural problem of the company. In their opinion, the owner of GM, who was basically a "real good guy," would not have tolerated the injustices the manager imposed on its workforce.

Another impetus for building an organizing campaign was the introduction of the second line into the production process. Eighty percent of the employees I interviewed claimed that implementing Line Two was the reason they felt a union was necessary. With the arrival of Line Two, several labor problems occurred. First, employees could no longer control their time at work. Workers were forced to miss their breaks and lunches to attend to the lines. More consequential, employees were forced to stay after their twelve-and-one-quarter-hour shifts to bale the waste caused by the many unresolved kinks in Line Two. Baling waste consisted of disposing of inferior material that the company would be unable to sell. Second, workers, both black and white, were not getting evaluations, were not moving up in skill level, and therefore were not receiving raises. Finally, workers, especially black employees, argued that discrimination was exacerbated with the appearance of the second line. For example, black workers were less likely than white workers to be given time off from baling waste if they had a pressing engagement after their scheduled work hours. One white employee summed up the situation:

> When I first worked there, it was unreal the way people were being treated. Besides open racism, they were working twelve hours and if you got a break, that was fine. If you didn't, that was fine too. If you got evaluated that was fine, and if you didn't that was fine too. The way they looked at it is "We pay you to do what we want you to do." That's one reason we brought a union in. Basically, that was the whole reason we started getting together. (8)

Before the workers could "bring the union in," however, they had to first win the election.

During the six-week campaign period, only one paid union organizer, Steve, remained continuously in the small Alabama town. However, union representatives from the regional and district offices came occasionally to help him. Steve stayed in one of the two motels in the area, approximately four miles from GM. Having the organizer located so close to the workplace gave employees a place to congregate. The average GM employee lived thirty minutes from the plant, making it difficult for co-workers to meet. The organizing campaign, however, gave many employees both a reason and a place to meet. One African-American worker said:

> Sometimes I would go to Steve's after work just to see what was happening and hear the latest news. There'd be three or four people hanging out, maybe writing fliers, maybe just talking. It was a fun time because everyone was involved. (12)

Also, Steve's proximity to the plant allowed him to disseminate information among the workers effectively. He acted much like a central information center, linking together workers in different departments and on different shifts. As the same employee continued:

> Steve always knew what was going down. We'd just go on over to the motel after work and hear what was happening to everybody else. Then we'd pass the information on. Everything that went on you knew about. It was easy to find out about. If you didn't know you could call somebody because everybody knew what was going on all the time.

Some employees trusted the organizer from the beginning, believing that his motives for helping to unionize the company stemmed strictly from a concern for exploited workers. One white worker stated, "There's no way they can be making anything off of our dues money, so they must have been interested." (4)

Most employees, however, claimed that their trust in the organizer grew over time. Three conditions fostered their confidence in the union. First, from time to time, the union brought union workers from nearby companies to converse with GM employees. Speaking with workers who had dealt with the union before made GM employees trust that the union made reasonable claims. Second, four workers said that they performed independent "research" about unions. These workers had no experience with unions prior to the organizing campaign and felt compelled to do their own investigations[5] to avoid getting swept away into a movement that they little understood. One white technician said:

> Before I was willing to jump on the bandwagon I did a little research. I went to the library and read about unions and then I'd talk to some of my

personal friends that were in management. I come to find out that the union was telling more truth than the company was and so I trusted the organizers. (19)

Third, and most importantly, the organizer was able to predict what actions the company would take to squash the organizing campaign. This ability to foresee GM's behavior demonstrated to the workforce that Steve was competent, legitimate, and honest. As these technicians explained:

> *African-American Technician:* When we went in, Steve was upfront and he would tell us how they were going to try to break us up racially, where they were going to try to tell us that the union was bad. Everything that he told us would happen about how the company would handle this thing, did happen. It's happening now. He said, once we win, not if, but once we win, the fight is just going to be started. He said, they're going to take union officials, put them in other jobs, just to kill that voice if it's strong and all the things he said happened. (2)

> *White Technician:* They predicted just about everything the company was going to do, I imagine, about word for word. You'd go in one day and you would see something, and they would have talked about the same thing the night before at a meeting. (8)

> *White Technician:* They sat down and talked with you about some of the things that you could expect and the company would do and the tactics that the company would use. I give them credit, they knew what was coming up and that was a benefit to them. (13)

Organizers and workers established trust, then, through their interactions during the campaign.

The clothing workers' union depended on the workers in the plant to attain union success. Employee participation was established, first, through creation of a workers' committee. The committee at GM consisted of a core group of twelve people who were responsible for organizing and motivating fellow workers, as well as establishing strategy.[6] A committee member differed from a regular, participant employee in the amount of time and responsibility dedicated to the organizing campaign. A committee member consistently went to Steve's motel after or before work, helped organize the content of fliers and weekly meetings, and spoke up at the plant when the company spoke adversely about unions. Committee members believed that workers shared with Steve the responsibility of organizing the workplace. Two committee members described their activity:

> *African-American Technician:* I suggested quite a few things during the campaign. Like we couldn't meet all at one time, so I suggested we meet

at different times. And I picked the motel the organizer stayed at because the president stays at the one hotel so we suggested the other hotel. We suggested who he should met with and when. I would come and tell him who was for the union and who wasn't 'cause some people just weren't for it. He wouldn't go to the guys that weren't for the union. We would write things that we would like changed and he would print them up and put them in pamphlets and stuff. People would keep the pamphlets and read them and some workers pinned them to the wall in the plant and the company would put out their own pamphlet. I played a great part of the campaign, I did. I was really more of an organizer than the guy they had down here 'cause I had the workers outside and inside the plant. (1)

White Technician: I would go over to Steve's hotel every day and fill him in on what happened during the day: who lost their temper, who was trying to say what to the people. I'd give him an update on the day's progress, tell him the attitudes of the people. And we'd try to figure out what needed to be done and presented as far as handouts. We'd try to counter what had been posted by the company. The company was running an antiunion campaign by posting certain literature. We'd have a skull session and counter the lit. and pass them out to people the next day. We basically worked together, but sometimes there was different viewpoints. But we worked it out. We'd sit and talk about them and work out the best possible scenario. (5)

Committee members provided two types of information that helped educate their fellow employees about unionism. The first involved strategy that the company would utilize to break the workers apart, such as telling employees that unions force companies to go out of business or take all the workers' money as dues. The second type of information given to co-workers was about what a union could do for GM employees:

African-American Organizing Committee Member: Steve told us from the beginning that the Constitution gave us rights as citizens, but as workers we have no rights, and that's just not fair. . . . He said that only by working together could we create a strong union. We are the union, and together we could make any changes we wanted. And that's just what I told my co-workers. (1)

The organizer conveyed to GM employees that the union was the worker, and that to win the election workers must be united. Workers, then, placed pressure on each other to become active in the campaign. While committee members did not expect their co-workers to help plan strategy, they did expect them to attend meetings, go to social functions, and help talk their co-workers into signing union cards. As a result, everyone I interviewed attended at least one union meeting and fifteen of the twenty attended at least five union meetings.[7] Furthermore, the same fifteen who attended at least five union meetings also participated in the picnics and barbecues and talked to people on their shift about joining the union.[8]

Unlike the organizers at BGS, Steve did not have access to the workplace. He could only talk to workers if he found them at home or if they came to his motel. In fact, much of his time was spent driving around the rural area from one home to another, attempting to speak to workers. Rarely, the strategy of visiting workers' homes was not well received. A white worker who defined himself as ambivalent towards the union remembered:

> I didn't appreciate him coming to my home at all. He didn't even call. I was doing just fine talking to the other men at work. I know them. I don't know him from Adam. (18)

Given that Steve had no access to the plant, GM employees, both committee members and others, became invaluable at disseminating information about the union to co-workers and at establishing the union as a trustworthy organization. They did this by talking to workers at the plant and/or convincing workers to attend the weekly union meetings held at Steve's motel room. Having employees talk to their co-workers helped establish the union efforts as legitimate.

Employees also were active inside the plant by countering any false information that GM was spreading. For instance, one worker (who did not define himself as ''active'') recalled that the company told employees that the union forced workers at a company in another county to strike, which compelled the plant to close. He said:

> The company had a lot of facts. I'll tell you one for instance. They told us how the union voted in the plant in Georgina and the plant went out of business.
> *Interviewer: And it was because of the union?*
> In a way. Once the union got in there, the workers felt they had a lot of job security and they got to the point where they really didn't want to do their job. They slipped in quality and the company went out of business. But a year after that—and they [Geofelt] didn't show us this part: I had to research this part myself—the union went out and found a buyer to buy the plant and re-opened it. They came in with higher wages and better benefits and they're still open. But they [Geofelt] didn't tell us that, I had to tell them that and it was real interesting. It was fun to tell them they were wrong. (3)

Organizing the workplace, then, happened both within the plant and outside it. Their collective action, workers believed, not only facilitated a successful organizing campaign, but also brought them closer together. One of the least active workers I interviewed, an African-American technician who never committed himself to the union, still admitted:

> There was no one really in charge of the campaign. I just know that some workers were a little more active than others. I can't say anybody was in charge. And I think that brought us closer together in thought and in feelings, as far as closeness, and that now we can stand together. We can fight together. If something happens to you I'll be there, that type of effect. (15)

Another employee, an active white technician, said:

> During the campaign, we just pulled together like I've never seen anyone pull together. We actually became a team. They always talk about a team, but we never had a team until the union organizers came and pulled us together. We were actually a family and a team. (4)

Although employees strengthened their unity during the campaign, most workers admitted that the campaign created two distinct camps: those for the union and those against. The simple division strengthened the bonds of people within each camp.

Unlike BGS, GM responded to its workers organizing with an antiunion campaign. Geofelt hired a lawyer specializing in labor-management relations to help persuade employees that a union was unnecessary. The first strategy of the company involved acts of contrition. As one worker stated:

> When the union first came up, damn! We got raises, we got breaks, lunch. And our supervisor was real nice for about a month. (7)

The company president and vice-president came to the plant and talked personally with each worker. The company's attempt at reform was convincing to a few people, such as the young African-American worker mentioned above who had previously enjoyed showing the company it was wrong. He explained, "I didn't think we needed a union because the company had changed" (3). He eventually voted against the union, even while his co-workers believed he was "pro." However, most workers did not "buy" the sudden shift.

After contrition failed to stop the organizing campaign, the company began an information bombardment. Workers were a captive audience at meetings where they were told that unions only desired money and were third parties that would harm the company. At one meeting, a manager read from a union handbook how the union would fine each employee large sums of money if they did not participate in any strike called by the union. A member of the organizing committee proudly recalled:

> I got my own little book out and found the same phrase and read it directly. It basically said that the only people who could call the strike are the workers at the plant. The bosses got real mad at me. (1)

In fact, the meetings did more harm for the antiunion campaign than good. The common meeting area inside the plant gave workers time to build solidarity and talk to workers sitting on the fence. The company realized its mistake quickly and never scheduled a group meeting again.

The rumor that was most effective at scaring employees was that the union would force GM workers to give up their excellent health insurance in exchange for the union's mediocre plan. With employee encouragement, regional union officials quickly had certificates made stating that the union would not force workers to take the union insurance plan. Employees brought certificates into GM the next week and handed them out to workers. One worker said that he snuck one onto the desk of his supervisor, who very openly tore it up.

As the campaign election grew closer, the company engaged in yet another strategy: divide and conquer. Employees were taken off the line one by one for private meetings with supervisors. White workers were told that black workers would take over the company if the union came in. Black workers were told that a union would only harm the company financially. Also, employees were kept from speaking with each other. Only one employee from each shift at a given time was allowed off the line for lunch or breaks. And one white worker, a member of the organizing committee known for his vociferous pro-union stance, was taken off the line altogether and placed into an isolated area. An active white worker recalled:

> They were hard on the people that was really for the union. Like Jones, they stuck him out in the warehouse by himself one day so he wouldn't be able to talk to anyone. They didn't want nobody to speak to anyone about the union. If there were like two or three of us together they'd split us up. (8)

Employees of GM countered the divide-and-conquer technique by engaging in social activities, like Sunday family barbecues and after-work parties. Getting together with their families outside of work successfully allowed employees to overcome any isolation that they may have faced at work.

Besides the antiunion campaign begun by the company, five workers also joined together to protest the union's efforts. These five workers claimed to be completely independent from the company (although prounion workers believed that they were guided by GM management).[9] They were not, however, as organized as the company. Their antiunion efforts were sporadic and consisted mostly of speaking to co-workers negatively about unions. Yet despite their disorganization, the antiunion campaign wielded an effective tool at dissuading ambivalent workers. A woman from the lab had previously been in the same union at a different plant. She claimed that while she was pregnant the union failed to pay her bills, leaving her with a high debt that she was still paying off. The prounion folks brought this fact to the attention of the organizer, and, after some research, the union paid the bill. Regardless of why the problem existed, some workers interpreted the union suspiciously after the woman's story spread.

One time, the five antiunion workers, all white, "crashed" a union meeting being held at Steve's. One of the antiunion people recalled:

> We went in the meeting and began firing all these questions at him, and he couldn't answer any of them. I knew he wouldn't be able to. He was telling us that the union could make things better at the workplace. But I knew that was a lie, and besides, things were already going great. (17)

The one similarity that pro- and antiunion employees shared was a belief that their actions in the campaign mattered. As the same antiunion employee stated, "I knew that the organizing campaign was only going to go in my direction if I put time into it" (17). While the two camps were working towards different ends, they felt confident that their struggles would sway the campaign outcome.

Despite the endeavors of the five workers and the company, the union campaign resulted in favor of the union, with sixty out of the seventy workers voting "yes." Employees felt that a union would herald changes at GM that would benefit both the workers and the company.

Conclusion

Most of the workers at both BGS and GM wanted union representation, since management had instigated changes that increased worker
responsibility in the companies and lowered morale. Yet the process
of unionization differed at BGS and GM. Organizers conveyed to BGS
employees that they held a passive role in the campaign; organizers
would bring the union in and workers would accrue the benefits. The
only participation needed by BGS workers, then, was a payment of
union dues once the union succeeded in attaining a contract. Workers
of GM, on the other hand, were taught to actively participate in the
creation of a union. Organizers conveyed to GM workers that only
through a united group could there be the desired transformation at
the company. In the next chapter, I discuss how the social context of
organizing shaped both the meaning workers derived from the campaigns and, subsequently, the workers' emotional and ideological responses to the unions.

5

Building Union Frameworks

A Union Employee at Bob's: The union was trying to sell us, trying to convince us to sign solicitation cards, but I never even signed a solicitation card because it seemed like all they were signing in were carry-outs. They didn't try to get long-term employees. That really turned me off. Then all of sudden Bob's decided that because of PR, publicity, we will bargain with these people. I guess Bob's decided it was time to go with the flow, Taylor's has a union, Food-for-Cheap has a union. I don't know, but the powers that be decided that we should go with the flow. That's how we became union. (22)

A Union Employee at Geofelt: I think during the campaign, we put away a lot of our little problems, bickering. I got a chance to meet guys and talk to guys that I knew were there but did not know. Ah, people worked together, they welcomed each other into their homes and we just felt stronger, like we could get something done. It was kind of like building a family relationship thing. We all realized we were fighting for one common cause, job security for everyone. We became closer. You could sit down and drink coffee and tea with them and they might pour their heart out to you, whereas normally you just ignored each other and you normally just didn't care. And you realized you were all the same, just worried about making a living and keeping your job. (3)

Introduction

Goffman's "frame analysis" describes how the social context of organizing exposes workers to symbols that influence the way workers interpret reality. This suggests that action cannot be studied wholly outside the context in which it occurs. The purpose of an organizing campaign, for example, is to successfully unionize a workplace. Yet the way organizers interact with workers to bring about success generates meaning that ultimately connects symbols with behavior.

My view is that the interactions workers had with the unions during the organizing campaigns shaped the likelihood of action. The Comprehensive Campaign at Bob's Grocery Stores (BGS) represents a more traditional, authoritarian institutional arrangement. The quote from the BGS worker that begins this chapter aptly illustrates how the organizing context included "the powers that be" and excluded worker activism. Indeed, during the Comprehensive Campaign, organizers approached employees primarily to convince them to sign union authorization cards. In most cases, persuasion took the form of promising workers that, in exchange for union dues, the union would provide individual workers with better benefits and wages than those they presently received. These limited interactions encouraged a "union as business" framework: workers understood and acted towards the union as if they had no room to participate except within the business transaction.

The Blitz campaign at Geofelt Manufacturing (GM) exemplifies better the alternative, institutional arrangement that Pateman views as generating people's sense of efficacy and activism. The quote from the GM worker at the beginning of this chapter characterizes how imperative workers perceived their activism was in establishing unity during the clothing workers' campaign. In fact, workers experiencing the Blitz did have control in deciding the development of their campaign. Employees met together regularly with the organizer to create literature, discuss strategy, and build cohesion. These interactions encouraged solidarity among co-workers and promoted a "union as workers" framework: workers united with the understanding that success was the responsibility of the workforce as a whole.

The participatory theory of democracy, combined with Goffman's "frame analysis," further asserts that the meaning workers derive from participating in an active democracy will emotionally and ideologically transform them. As individuals interact within participatory institutional arrangements, they are likely to develop emotional benefits such as enhanced organizational satisfaction and increased self-efficacy (Mason 1982; Pateman 1970). Furthermore, the meanings workers construct from participatory democratic organizations are likely to foster a culture of solidarity in which group ideologies emerge rather than individual ones (Greenberg 1986; Pateman 1970).

The purpose of this chapter is twofold. First, I link the levels of participatory democracy during the campaigns to the types of union frameworks employees generated. Second, I describe how different levels of activism during the BGS and GM campaigns, together with the creation of union frameworks, influenced workers' sentiments, feelings of efficacy, and creation of union ideology.

The "Union as Business" Framework at Bob's Grocery Stores: Withholding Information, Communication, and Decision-Making

Several related aspects of the BGS campaign discouraged workers from participating in organizing efforts and served to foster a "union as business" framework. First, regional and international union leaders controlled the course of the campaign, deciding how to implement strategy and assigning the players to their tasks. When the Comprehensive Campaign became the chosen tactic, union leaders felt that it was imperative to keep details about the campaign secret from workers and organizers. The less the company knew about the union's strategy, the more the information could be used to convince BGS to recognize the union. While withholding strategy from workers aided in effectively surprising the company, it also kept employees from actively helping the union gain entry into the workplace. Indeed, organizers controlled who and how many workers were permitted to participate; only eight workers from the grocery side of BGS became active. When organizers did ask other employees to participate, it was simply to demand help in procuring union cards. They sought no input with regards to union strategy. Since the union did not provide workers information about campaign strategy, employees had little opportunity to communicate their opinions to organizers or to share in decision-making.

Second, campaign leaders made it clear to organizers that their main goal inside the stores was to collect as many signatures from workers as possible. In order to accomplish this end, organizers did not spend time establishing trust and rapport with the workers, although they had access to employees inside the stores. Rather, encounters were often brief and ended after the employee signed a union authorization card. To entice employees to sign cards, organizers often made promises that the union would improve working conditions. Sometimes organizers made questionable promises, for example claiming that workers would receive monetary bonuses when the union became the representative of the workplace. In all cases, organizers made it clear that, after the union gained entry, employees simply had to pay union dues in order to attain better wages and benefits.

Third, organizers did not encourage collective mobilization among workers during the campaign. Commonly, unions establish meetings for workers during campaigns to invoke solidarity among them. However, even though the union had enough organizers to rally chain-wide support, there were no store or chain-wide meetings during the entire twenty-month campaign at BGS.

With limited access to participatory democracy during the campaign, workers were taught not to view activism as part of their role. One white cashier said:

> They [the union] knew how to do their job. They had brought these people in that had done this before. 'Cause I asked them if they needed help and they said, "This is our job and this is what we do. We are organizers." They knew what they were doing. (24)

Instead of participatory democracy, organizers emphasized getting union cards; this further convinced most workers that the union was not interested in employee participation. For instance, the worker I interviewed who had been active in the failed organizing campaign six years earlier did not participate in the successful campaign. He explained:

> I didn't participate in the campaign because I thought it was stupid. They were making all these promises they couldn't keep. I didn't take it seriously. But my first experience with the union was totally different, when it was secretive, and we'd meet at the union hall. That was good, that was a good experience for me because I knew they were serious. And we all got together to work out things. We could all relate. I kind of thought we were family there. We got together, and the union people were there, and Bob's employees were there, but they didn't do that this time. . . . This time, they just wanted us to sign cards. It was real obvious to me that they wanted us in there because of our numbers and we would bring in more money. (1)

Other union workers made similar comments about why they refrained from participating in the campaign.

> *Female Photo/Sound Clerk:* I didn't expect them to ask me about how to make the campaign effective. They were just more interested in getting people to sign on, and when they got the person to sign on, that's the last that you heard from them. I don't know what I expected from unions, not

being around them at all, but that's true. Once you signed on, that's the last you heard from them. (15)

Female Baker: They didn't really want us to get involved. They more just wanted to draw on the negative things Bob's had done, with the layoffs and stuff, and how they were going to save you from that. (18)

Interacting with organizers taught employees that the union's goal was obtaining signed union cards. Therefore, workers did not perceive participation as their responsibility. Instead, the union conveyed to employees that their role in the organizing campaign ended after they signed a card. Through the "professional" presentation-of-self, workers learned to view the union as a business organization specializing in union organizing and contract negotiations. Workers, then, began to perceive the union as a business. Indeed, 83 percent of the employees I interviewed compared the union to a business. As these four employees explain:

Union, Male Scanning Coordinator: I know that's how businesses work. You fool a few people, and then you get in. But I thought it [the campaign] was very shady. This union was very shady about a lot of things, about all the promises they were making, feeding the fire, giving false information about Bob's. (1)

Nonunion, Male Stocker: I think the union came in here for the money. It's big business, so I think they [employees] have to realize that. They have to realize that the union had other reasons for being there than just for their protection. Union did not come in because little old Sammy was getting fired. The union came in there for the money. (10)

Union, Male Stocker: I still don't know how the union got in so easy.
Interviewer: Is there someone you could ask?
Who could I ask? The company, the union? I think union negotiators, all those people in power, they're not in it for all the beautiful reasons. They're in it for the power and money. But, you know, those organizers were professional. They'll get you stuff. (28)

Union, Female Cashier: I think this union is in business exactly the same way we are. Only they're handling people, we're handling groceries. They're in it to make money. That was obvious from the start. The way they came in, we never knew what was going on, and all they wanted us to do was sign cards. They should be in it for the benefit of the people because a united group is obviously listened to more than an individual. But now that I know who they are, I'm just going to make sure we get our money's worth. As long as they're here and we're paying dues, then we'll make them work for us as much as we can. That's what we're paying them for, you know. (26)

Without shared information, communication, and decision-making, workers often saw their relationship with the union as a simple contractual relationship, one in which employees would pay the union dues in exchange for such benefits as job security and higher wages. The "business" concept of the union was cultivated by keeping strategy secret from workers and by limiting the types and frequency of interactions between organizers and employees. For the most part, workers accepted the union's business presentation-of-self. However, they did articulate one caveat stated succinctly by the worker active in the first organizing campaign. He warned, "I think the union should be careful that they're not so much like a business that they become like the businesses they're trying to better" (1).

The "Union as Workers" Framework at Geofelt Manufacturing: Producing Information, Communication, and Decision-Making

Worker participation in the GM campaign was the main ingredient that generated a "union as workers" framework among employees. As early as the initial canvassing for employee signatures, organizers made it clear that bringing the union into the workplace would take concerted effort among the employees. As a result, workers were crucial in establishing the campaign as legitimate and creating strategy. The organizer shaped a participatory campaign in three ways. First, he formed an organizing committee that consisted of 17 percent of the workforce. A very active group of twelve workers assisted in developing union fliers, planned and ran union meetings, and informed co-workers about the basics of a union. These people also introduced the paid organizer, Steve, to fellow employees who were ambivalent about and did not trust the union. As one member of the organizing committee said:

> The organizer did a lot of footwork when we were working, but it was definitely a joint effort. They couldn't organize us without help from the people and we couldn't get organized without help from them. (1)

Noncommittee employees also became active during the campaign. However, they limited their organizing efforts to attending weekly meetings, talking to co-workers inside the plant, attending (rather than planning) social activities, and occasionally riding around with the organizer. As one technician admitted about why he was active, "Because I just knew that if we had the majority of that plant the working conditions would be a lot better" (6).

Second, the organizer educated workers, both on and off the committee, about how to be "organizers." For instance, the organizer
informed workers not to develop interactions that "pressured" employees into signing authorization cards. An active, African-American
worker from the shipping department said:

> The guy told us not to try to force something on any of them. Just put it
> out there, and if they want it, give it to them. . . . if not, go ahead on about
> your business. If they ask you a question, answer it to the best that you
> can. If you can't answer it, then you get back with them and call me and
> I'll give you an answer, then you can explain it to them. (12)

A nonactive, white technician confirmed this strategy:

> There was a couple of co-workers that came around and would talk to me,
> trying to win me over to their side of thinking about it. There wasn't that
> much negativity about it. They just tried to point out the pros, I guess, of
> the union. A couple of guys talked to me like that, but there really wasn't
> any pressure in the situation. (18)

Although the organizer dissuaded workers from pressuring their co-
workers to join the organizing efforts, some employees did feel co-
erced into being active. The pressure workers experienced, however,
came from other co-workers, not from the organizer. One African-
American technician recalled the pressure he received from his co-
workers during the campaign:

> The ones that were really involved sort of put pressure on you. There's
> always going to be some type of leaders and people that are really into
> that. The ones that were really into it would come up to me and talk to
> me and try to convince me about being part of the union. They were into
> getting the whole shift behind the union so I felt pressured into going to a
> couple of meetings. They'd try to tell me that we can get this and we can
> get that, if we all stick together. (15)

Ultimately, the belief of active workers that only through their collective endeavors could they make changes at the workplace justified
why they pressured co-workers to participate.

The organizer also warned employees to refrain from making promises about monetary benefits. The only promise Steve made to workers
was that, if GM employees stood together, work conditions would
certainly change. An active African-American worker explained:

> He told us that with us fighting together it will be better, that's all we can
> promise anyone. We just wanted to make people believe that the union
> could help and that they just needed to have faith. I could make promises

and I'm going to try to show you it's best to sign a card, vote yes, but I don't have a damn thing to give you except hope that something might change if we all work together. (2)

This refusal to try to "sell" workers the union stands in sharp contrast to the strategy employed at BGS.

The final way the organizer solicited employee participation during the campaign was through inciting collective mobilization. Steve informed workers that the campaign would only be successful if the workers joined together. Collective action, he told them, could overcome their fear, create solidarity, and generate positive change in the workplace. A young, white technician who described himself as semi-active explained:

I learned during the campaign that workers have rights. They don't have to take everything that's dished out to them. If people stick together they can get more out of a group than they can out of being solo. You have more chance of achieving what you want 'cause as long as we stick together we can really do something there. It's going to be more profitable for everyone. 'Cause if you just, if you don't take pride in your work, then you just ain't going to work that hard, and you're not going to make profit.
Interviewer: How will this make you have pride in your work?
Because everybody will stick together, have pride in each other. Therefore they'll eventually start taking pride in their work. Better atmosphere and you'll start taking pride in your work.
Interviewer: Were you all together before the campaign?
Well, kind of, it was different. We might make a joke together, but as far as sticking together if something was going on, you know, not really.
Interviewer: And that changed during the campaign?
Yeah, I believe it did. We all tried to communicate about work and what we wanted. We tried to stick up for each other and realized that we're all working for the same things. You know, so if I see someone who hasn't had a break and they haven't had one I'll go break them off and I wouldn't have done that before.
Interviewer: Why not?
I just didn't think about what they were going through before. You just kind of thought of yourself. I guess I think about the others more now. Everybody's working together getting the job done, and that's helping the company. (8)

As a result of invoking their own sense of community, workers learned to view each other in a new light, a light that illuminated the importance of employee unity. Furthermore, workers viewed solidarity as instrumental not only for winning the campaign, but also for making the workplace more efficient.

The participatory democratic structure during the campaign generated an attitude among GM employees that worker participation was, first and foremost, their right. One African-American technician on the union committee said, "People aren't going to be satisfied unless they have some say-so" (1). The participatory structure also taught workers that participation was their responsibility. One African-American technician said, "If you ever want to better yourself, you've got to fight sometimes. It's just like anything else. Nothing in life is free" (2). Given that workers viewed participation as both their right and their responsibility, the active prounion GM employees treated the issue of their participation as nonproblematic. They did not ask, "Should I participate or not?" They asked, "Do I want a union or not?" Indeed, one white employee answered when I asked him what motivated him to participate, "What do you mean? If I didn't participate, how would we have gotten organized?" (10)

Antiunion workers also believed that their actions in the campaign were essential at affecting the election outcome. Since they, too, surmised that a union was defined by its members, they felt it was their duty to inform GM employees about why a union was not necessary at the workplace. They did this primarily by talking to their co-workers on the job. For instance, a woman in the lab said, "I was active because I didn't want to be governed by a union. I didn't want to live by their rules." (20) A male employee active in the antiunion campaign said:

> So, I let it be known how I felt because I knew things would be worse, and I told them how they'd have to follow someone else's rules with the union. That's what I let be known to people, I thought it was at least my duty to let them know. (17)

The image of the union as something only a united group of workers could create or, for that matter, deny led employees to develop a "union as workers" framework. Seventy-five percent of the employees spoke of the union as an organization of active workers. One technician claimed:

> We knew that the only way to change things at Geofelt was by joining together. In numbers you have strength. Any union is only as strong as its people. That's what Steve told us and that's what I believe. (4)

This "workers" conception resulted from employees educating themselves and their co-workers about unionism and from acting together to create (or destroy) a union.

Union Frameworks and Satisfaction, Efficacy, and Ideology During the Campaigns

The "Union as Business" Framework at Bob's Grocery Stores

The creation of a "union as business" framework at BGS stemmed mostly from the encounters workers had with organizers. Workers described organizers as "salesmen" interested in "only getting cards signed" to "make money." Indeed, one nonunion cashier insisted on replacing the word "organizer" with "salesman" during his entire interview (16). Being seen as salesmen, as they were by 77 percent of the interviewed employees, did not endear the organizers to BGS workers. As one union, female merchandise clerk stated:

> They're just too pushy, they're like salesmen. You know when you try to buy a car, they lock you in a room and they won't let you out. They're pushy and won't take no for an answer.
> *Interviewer: What are they trying to sell?*
> The union and all their benefits. To me, they're just an overbearing salesman. (3)

The profession of "salesman" does not inherently embody negative characteristics. Salesmen can be assertive and knowledgeable. Employees of BGS who compared organizers to a salesperson, however, used the analogy in a pejorative way, as the following employees explained:

> *Nonunion, Female Merchandise Clerk:* I didn't like them. They were pushy. And you know what they remind you of, door to door salesmen that won't leave. And that's exactly what they were. They would come and they would not leave until. . . . They had people at the break table with these stupid forms saying, "All you got to do, is sign right here, sign right here." And they wouldn't leave until people signed. Bull! Just get away from me and leave me your packet and I'll read it. And that's where people need to realize this is the nineties. You have to have backbone. You have to speak up for yourselves 'cause nobody's going to speak up for you. (29)
> *Nonunion, Male Cashier:* I mean the blind faith these people had in the union. I mean they voted on a contract they never even saw. They put so much trust in them. They [the organizers]'re like snake oil salesmen. They sold them something they couldn't even see and they voted on it. And they're paying for it. (16)
> *Union, Female Cashier:* I wasn't impressed with them. I felt like they were trying to, like a salesman, trying to push something on you that you don't

> want. They were trying to manipulate you. I didn't trust them. I felt like
> they were trying to pressure me into something. (9)

Ninety percent of BGS employees described organizers as "pushy"
in their attempts to persuade workers to sign union cards. Employees
claimed organizers "bothered" workers at the stores, "selling the
union" at the snack bar while employees were taking breaks or in the
aisles while they were working. A young, female carry-out exclaimed,
"I don't know, they [organizers] just bugged you. I finally just signed
a card, so they'd leave me alone." (11) Indeed, employees claimed
that the day they signed the union card was often the last they ever
spoke with the organizers. A union female clerk in the photo/sound
department said:

> They were just more interested in getting people to sign on, and when they
> got the person to sign on that was the last that you heard from them. I
> don't know what I expected from unions given that I have never been
> around them. But it was true. Once you signed on, that was the last you
> heard from them.
>
> *Interviewer: How did that make you feel?*
> Like a fool. (15)

Workers felt pressure from organizers to sign cards. Once they signed
the card, many felt abandoned.

Seventeen percent of the workers I interviewed further claimed that
their positive image of unions had been harmed by the organizing
campaign. One woman began the interview with a very negative attitude towards unions, which I wrongly assumed had been formed
prior to the organizing campaign. During the interview she surprised
me by revealing that she used to be prounion. I asked her to explain:

> The union was able to go to the main office, get everybody's address, and
> start sending them propaganda. I ignored it at first because I didn't think
> we would actually allow ourselves to have a union because we never had
> before. Because we tried to do it like five years ago, and believe it or not,
> I was actually excited about it.
>
> *Interviewer: Tell me about that.*
> Nobody would talk about it 'cause they were afraid we'd get fired, and I
> was like, "No, we should have a union, we don't have insurance, we don't
> get paid, we need more money." But then nobody contacted me about it.
> It was like just word of mouth, I don't even think the union people were
> around. I just think Bob's employees brought it up. . . .
>
> *Interviewer: So what changed your mind about unions?*
> The way they came in. You know, I'm up there doing my job and some

guy is trying to talk to me. He's saying, "Here, take this and read it," being all pushy. And I'm like, "I don't want it." He doesn't listen: "Just take it and read it." But I don't want it. Finally to shut the guy up I took it and threw it in the garbage basket right there. The organizers would go in the back rooms, a fight almost ensued. They were so pushy. Needless to say, we called the police and got them out of there, and that's when we got definite guidelines about where they could go and if they didn't follow those guidelines we would have them arrested. (14)

The woman was not disappointed that a union tried to organize BGS; she was dissatisfied that the organizers "pushed" themselves on employees in their attempt to organize the company.

Employees stated they developed a negative stereotype about organizers for another reason besides their "pushiness." Organizers seemed principally focused on simply procuring union cards. Long-term employees explained that organizers were obviously only interested in getting union cards signed because they targeted carry-outs as opposed to "real employees." Carry-outs are the employees who bag groceries, collect grocery carts, and help bring groceries to the customer's car. They tend to be part-timers of high-school age. While carry-outs make up the largest job category in grocery stores, they frequently have short job tenures. Thirty-three percent of the interviewed BGS employees complained that organizers spent "too much time" trying to organize carry-outs. In the words of one union, male stocker:

Back in the old days, you knew the shop steward, you knew what they represented. Out here it's strictly a mind game. It's organization. I mean when these guys that came in, they were organizing carry-outs, who don't know what a union is or what they are representing. They were just looking for dollars. If the organizers had come in and were going after ten-, fifteen-year employees I would have respected that because we are the people who will be represented. But you tell these nineteen-, twenty-year-olds they're going to get a buck an hour more and sure, they're going to sign a card. (22)

For employees with seniority, "going after" carry-outs was tantamount to organizers admitting that they were "not interested in the employees, just in getting union cards signed." This portrait of organizers left many employees, even carry-outs, disappointed with the union.

One young carry-out told me that before the organizing campaign she was very prounion, believing that unions were the "voice" of

employees. Both her parents were union members, her father the steward in his. Yet she admitted that the union campaign at BGS dramatically altered her opinion about labor unions:

> At school we learned that unions were good. But the one at work really
> taught me a lot about unions. I used to be prounion but now I'm not. I
> always thought it was for employee rights. But all they did was bug you,
> wanting you to sign a card. That's all they wanted. (11)

The salient feature of the campaign that changed this carry-out's opinion was the organizers' drive to collect union cards.

Other workers also expressed irritation that organizers seemed
mostly motivated to gather cards. Three white, male stockers commented:

> *Union Stocker:* They say, "Hey, why don't you come back and sign this
> card that says that you are just considering joining the union, it just indi-
> cates to management that there are people interested in what the union has
> to say." Whatever they needed to tell you they would tell you just to get
> you to sign a card and I just wasn't interested and then I would get the
> cold shoulder from them. (7)
>
> *Nonunion Stocker:* I realize they were just saying stuff to get people to
> sign the little cards. They had people come from New York. I'd ask him
> a question and he didn't have a clue. I asked him, "Well, then why are
> you here?" He said, "We're here to drum up union support." I was like,
> ok, fine. But that tripped me out. (8)
>
> *Union Stocker:* I really don't think they came in with a lot of profession-
> alism. They came in, like I said, and had the attitude of "You on the
> payroll? Then sign this card. We want that card." They were just looking
> for the 51 percent. My personal opinion, they should have said, "We want
> you in the union for another twenty years, not just for the first three
> months." (22)

Most employees believed the union would have gained more support
if the organizers had acted less pushy and more honest. Two BGS
workers explained:

> *Nonunion, Female Carry-out:* The union should have approached people
> in a better way. I mean not bugging people. Most people thought they were
> a bother. They just didn't seem very sincere . . . you know? Maybe they
> should have had group meetings or something where there was a bunch of
> people at once, not just one on one. That would have made them seem
> more for the employee. (11)
>
> *Nonunion, Male Stocker:* I think their primary goal should have been to
> come in on the up and up and truly be the union that they represented
> themselves to be. It's supposed to be a union for the employee, yet they

hid too much from the employee. I think they lost a lot of trust and faith from a lot of these employees already. And they wouldn't have to deal with that if they came in with the goal and presented themselves as they were in their entirety and had taken their best shot that way. I think now, they hurt a little bit in their unity because of the way they came in. (10)

Workers interpreted the tactics used by organizers as self-interested rather than employee-centered and, as a result, the BGS employees I interviewed did not feel satisfied with the process of the campaign.

Yet another strategy exacerbated the impression that the union was mainly interested in procuring union cards: organizers sometimes exaggerated the benefits of a union to workers. Employees called these exaggerations "false campaign promises." Common examples of "campaign promises" included telling workers that: (1) signing a card simply meant that they wanted to vote on a union, (2) there would be a union election so that they could vote on a union, (3) they would get to decide what the contract said before they voted on the contract, and (4) the union could ensure employees their job security. Twenty percent of the employees also said that they were told or knew someone else who was told that employees who signed a card would receive a cash bonus when the union successfully became the bargaining agent at BGS. One nonunion, female customer-service representative claimed:

They promised people a one-hundred-dollar bonus if they joined the union. They also didn't tell people they would have to pay union dues. I really just don't think they gave them a clear understanding of what the union was going to do. They just said, "With us, you'll never get fired." And of course, these young kids believed every word. (14)

Campaign promises enticed some workers to sign union cards and join the union. However, 50 percent of the employees I interviewed said the promises were duplicitous and deeply harmed the sense of trust employees felt towards the union. Ultimately, organizers' "questionable" tactics reinforced the image with which most workers were dissatisfied, the image of the union as a business.

Throughout my interviews with workers, they clearly conveyed that they did not like feeling pressured or pushed into the union by organizers. Another outcome of the union-controlled campaign was that workers felt completely powerless over the organizing process. Indeed, workers felt inefficacious at the most fundamental level: they could not explain how the union "won" the campaign at BGS.

Most workers admitted that they found out about the union's success one day at work. One union cashier described her experience, a typical one:

> We didn't hear much about the union until we got the letter. The letter said that if the majority of the employees wanted the union, they could come in. And I was like, I haven't even heard of the union in like a year. So I was surprised. (6)

The letter posted by the company conveyed that workers could be represented by the union if they so desired. Yet neither the company nor the union clearly communicated to workers that the union already represented BGS employees. Once the company agreed to recognize the union, the signed authorization cards secured the union's success. Workers at BGS, then, were left to create an understanding of the campaign success for themselves. The account that workers generated to explain the union's success often depicted the grocery employees as passive and powerless victims of both the union and the company.

The most common story BGS employees invented to make sense of the campaign success was that about a union vote. Eighty-three percent of the workers with whom I spoke believed that the culmination of the campaign involved an election among workers, an election that involved, at most, corruption and, at least, little employee action. One nonunion, Latina cashier described her perception of what happened:

> *Interviewer: So people signed cards and then what?*
> There was a vote.
>
> *Interviewer: Who ended up voting?*
> I guess the employees.
>
> *Interviewer: But you didn't vote?*
> No, I didn't go to the meeting.
>
> *Interviewer: What made you decide not to vote either way?*
> Because I wasn't getting straight answers. It was difficult for me to vote for something I really didn't know about. Because as I understood it, making an appearance meant that you wanted to be part of the union.
>
> *Interviewer: Oh, really.*
> Yeah.
>
> *Interviewer: So if you didn't want the union, how were you able to demonstrate that?*
> Not go, just not go, as far as I understood it.
>
> *Interviewer: Was that explained to you at all?*
> Ah-eh, that was just something that was, I guess. (19)

Most notable in this cashier's comments is that she constructed an account of the union's success that gave her little power; the only way she felt capable of withdrawing her support was by *not* attending the "union vote."

The question to be answered is why most workers thought there was a union election when the union never held any meetings regarding the campaign. While the union held no group meetings, let alone an election, during the campaign process, it did hold several meetings about the contract negotiations after the union was recognized by BGS management. Workers at BGS confused the purpose of the contract meetings. They believed that the meetings were about an election for union recognition. Clearly, the election they attended or heard about was not a democratic one. Two BGS employees explain:

> *White, Male, Nonunion Cashier:* They had several meetings at hotels around the valley. I didn't go, but I talked to people that went. It was a huge meeting room where they rallied, like a motivational rally. There were people up there talking to the group, like, "You're going to have a better way of life." "Yeah!" "You're going to have more insurance." "Yeah!" "And by the way, let's vote now!" And they did it, heh. They did it with a show of hands, there was no private voting, no secret ballot. And there were several people who went, who didn't want the union. I guess it wasn't hands, it was standing. So they asked people who didn't want the union to stand up, and when these people stood up they were immediately surrounded by union people, like they ran to them. But this time it was three or four to one and they'd say, "What do you mean you came here and didn't want the union in?" Then they got rude and aggressive with the people I talked to, but that was only five-ten percent of the people. But it didn't faze anyone else because they got voted in. That's the strangest voting strategy I had ever heard, the old intimidation tactics again. Safety in numbers. There were a lot of people too, like one thousand at every place, and three or four meetings. (16)

Even employees who went to the "election" meeting were confused about what happened. As this worker explained:

> *White, Female, Union Cashier:* We had our meeting, after the cards had been accepted and it had been announced that we were going to have a union. We had a meeting, supposedly to vote on whether . . . but if you're not a member your vote's not valid anyway.
>
> *Interviewer: So only union members could vote on whether to accept the union?*
> Yes, and the meat department is already union, so they were the only ones that could vote on the union.
>
> *Interviewer: Really?*
> Yes. I went to the meeting and they asked us to vote by raising our hands.

> That's not legal. But the meat department had a closed ballot and they told us that they had already been accepted before they counted the closed ballots.
>
> *Interviewer: So was there a vote?*
> By the meat department, I think. (26)

Workers at BGS accepted that a "vote" for union recognition took place even when they could not explain when the election was held, who attended the meetings or how the vote transpired. Both the union and the company fostered the idea of a "vote" by failing to inform workers about the true nature of the campaign.

A second story that BGS workers created in an attempt to explain the union's entry into BGS involved corruption. Even when employees believed that a union election took place, they were suspicious about why the company finally agreed to a union when it was historically resistant to unions. Seventeen percent of the workers with whom I spoke reasoned that the union must have given the CEO an offer he couldn't refuse:

> *White, Male, Nonunion Stocker:* So there's been a lot of talk and you don't know how much rumor is true or not . . . but it wasn't that much after the president left the company that the union came in. And there's a lot of talk that there was money passed underneath the table to let the union in. (10)
>
> *White, Female, Union Merchandise Clerk:* When Bob's said they were finally going to have a vote for it, I thought to myself that the CEO had to have something lining his pockets for that to happen. And Bob's benefits from the union. Now they don't have to pay for medical, they don't have to worry about retirement. (12)

A side effect of keeping the campaign strategy secret was that employees created their own explanation about why the union withheld information. Some accounts made the union seem "shady." All accounts made the union seem authoritarian in its control of the campaign outcome. As a result, workers felt little efficacy.

The language that employees invoked to describe the union also demonstrates the limited self-efficacy workers experienced during the organizing campaign. First, none of the workers used the term "we" when discussing the union, only "they." In fact, 27 percent of the employees admitted that they did not even know the name of their union. When asked whom they were being represented by, one union cashier stated, "I have no idea, something about grocery stores or retail workers. I just don't know. Who cares as long as they do their job?" (24) Second, workers spoke of the union as if it were a third party, another institution to provide them rules rather than an organization controlled by themselves. A union stocker disappointed with the campaign said about the union:

> They're just the middlemen to fight for us at the main office and that's all they are. They don't work with us, they don't know what we're going through. All we can do is tell them, but they don't know if we're telling the truth or not and we don't know if they're telling us the truth or not because they're not in the stores. (5)

As a result of the distance between organizers and workers during the campaign, BGS workers saw the union as an outsider about whom they had little knowledge or control.

The authoritarian institutional arrangement of the BGS organizing campaign limited the types of interactions workers had with organizers; organizers promised workers that job security and other benefits could be established for interested employees in exchange for union dues. The message fostered by these interactions invoked a "union as business" framework. At the snackbar meetings, organizers discussed how having a union would give the employee job security, retirement, and more money. When one white cashier I interviewed told an organizer that she was not interested in the union, the organizer responded by asking, "Don't you want more money?" (9). Derivative from this business framework was an individualist ideology: BGS employees were taught to think of the union in self-interested terms. Workers asked, and were encouraged by organizers to ask themselves, "How will I benefit from the union coming in?" Two white, male BGS employees explained:

> *Union Stocker:* They were saying to me things that were best for me as an individual and that's the very first thing I realized. . . . I suppose if you probe it I guess you'd find out that I'm not too happy with the union. You know it hasn't done me any good and I don't want to take the "me" stance. There's too many people taking the "me" stance. The "me" stance doesn't do anybody any good, and it doesn't even do the "me's" any good. But they don't realize that. (7)

> *Union Steward:* I guess I would be more of a moderate. I see myself as more in the middle somewhere. I'm really not a big union person, that's why I don't really think I could go out there and push it and get people to sign up in the campaign. To each his own. I just know what they did for me, me personally. Why someone else signs it, or they don't join, they have totally different reasons than I do. (20)

Organizers encouraged BGS employees to evaluate the union using a cost-benefit analysis. The benefits of the union minus the cost of union dues equaled whether or not workers should sign a union card. Clearly, the union believed the majority of outcomes would be positive. Regardless of the outcome, however, the simple act of completing the equation taught workers much more than whether or not to sign a card. The equation also taught BGS workers that the decision was an individual problem to solve.

The "Union as Workers" Framework at Geofelt Manufacturing

The clothing workers' organizers told GM employees that they would have to act in concert to orchestrate a successful union election. Thus, the majority of workers involved themselves in creating change at the company. Employees first listened to the information that the organizers provided about unions and some did their own research to confirm that what the organizers said was accurate. Once workers believed that organizers gave them reliable information, they developed trust in the union, which gave them an impetus to join together and use the information in original ways to collectively mobilize the entire workforce. Both satisfaction and self-efficacy emerged through workers' concerted efforts to bring the union into GM. Indeed, activism was so closely linked with satisfaction and efficacy that workers often did not separate these concepts when they described their impressions of the campaign. One African-American technician recounted his experience:

> I wish you had a video camera during the campaign. I mean we were excited. And everyone went to the meetings after the shift and we felt together, like we knew what we were doing. And my shift had full participation. We were always going to the meetings. . . . It was real strong at first. For a while you could just walk through the plant and tell who was union and who wasn't. Everybody was always talking about the union and how we wanted things to change and how we were going to do it. We were all working to get things started, you know. And there were some people that were scared because we all value our jobs, but we got together and I felt really good. Me and a few other guys, we talked about how good we felt because when the union was first brought up, things were changing and I thought, "If just bringing it up could change things, what would happen if we got the union?" (7)

The "excitement" elicited during the campaign emerged from workers taking control over the campaign. Feeling self-efficacious, then, was partly how GM workers determined whether or not they were satisfied during the campaign.

A second source of satisfaction stemmed from workers' ability to establish unity. For instance, two employees said:

> *White Technician:* During the organizing campaign we just pulled together like I've never seen anyone pull together. We actually became a team. The company always talked about teams, but we never had one until the union organizers came and helped pull us together. (4)
>
> *African-American Technician:* The campaign brought us closer together. I guess by us being able to stand together, you know, we are closer. Now, we're involved, we're interacting together. Interacting has made us closer. (15)

Workers overcame obstacles that previously prevented them from coming together, and their ability to establish community made them proud and motivated to better the workplace. One white GM employee, for example, asserted that the unity established among union advocates extended beyond the circle of prounion workers. The technician explained that during the campaign his assistant supervisor, who was not part of the bargaining unit, occasionally needed help with a work-related problem:

> Well, we went to our assistant supervisor, he's not in the union, but he needed help a couple of times and we gave it to him. 'Cause it's a courtesy. And after we helped him we said, "See, this is how it will be with the union. See how we help each other?" (8)

On the whole, most workers admitted that two communities developed during the course of the campaign, those for the union and those against.

> *African-American, Union Warehouse Worker:* I think the union brought some of us together and pushed some of us apart. See, I had been in a union before so I wasn't as excited as these other guys. The ones that voted "no," the nonunion members, the guys just wouldn't leave them alone. And there was a lot of friction. I told them, "If a man don't want to join, just leave them alone." But no, they wouldn't leave them alone. They were trying to get every vote they could, and I think that pushed some people farther away. (9)
>
> *White, Antiunion Committee Technician:* For me, the workplace . . . it made it. . . . These employees, I work with them and they had no hard feelings for me and I had none against them and I've worked with them well all up to that time. Then all of a sudden here it was like a glass sheet separating us. They'd be talking and you standing right there and knowing they used

to talk to you and some of them just wouldn't talk to you. It made it hectic there. It was pretty bad up and down the line, conflict and tempers flared.

What is notable is that the problem nonunion employees had during the campaign was not with "pushy organizers," but with fellow workers, workers who admitted that creating solidarity enhanced their feelings of satisfaction and gave them a sense of efficacy.

When workers recalled the organizers, 65 percent said that most of their recollections were positive. For instance, they remembered how the organizers inspired motivation among employees and how they provided accurate and persuasive information. As this African-American technician explained:

> One of the organizers from Atlanta, I really liked him. He was a real motivator for me. He was very helpful 'cause he was a motivator. He knew what to say to get you motivated. Maybe what you wanted to hear, but it didn't come out that way. He was a little fellow, but he has some guts, man. If he told you, I'd go stand on this guy's toes and tell him blah, blah, blah, he'd do it.
>
> *Interviewer: How did he motivate you?*
> Well, when we went in, he was upfront and he would tell us how they were going to try to break us up racially, where they were going to try to tell us that the union was bad. Everything that he told us would happen about how the company would handle this thing did happen. It's happening now. He said, once we win, not if, but once we win, the fight is just going to be started. He said, "They're going to take union officials, put them in other jobs, just to kill that voice if it's strong." And all the things he said happened. (2)

However, most GM employees did not mention the organizers during the interviews until I asked them to discuss their relationship with them. In fact, workers' first memories of the campaign had more to do with their own activism and tenacity than with the organizers'. As one white technician said when I asked him to describe the campaign, "We finally said, 'Hey, we've had enough,' then it came together. We stood up and made a change" (19). Once again, the satisfaction generated within the campaign stemmed from workers' established community and their efficacy that grew from it.

Workers at GM attained efficacy through collectively mobilizing to establish a union. Ultimately, workers attributed the successful union outcome to their group efficacy. Four technicians described how imperative community was for the campaign's success:

> *White Technician:* What made the campaign effective was that we pulled together and pulled people we never thought we'd pull in. Like mainte-

nance, even though they didn't sign any cards, they voted three to one for the union; without their backing, it would have been very close. And the way we pulled them in was being able to stand together effectively to the corporation. When they published something, we'd counter the company with our facts. They never followed up their facts to counter our facts. So that raised a lot of questions in maintenance's mind. It gave us credibility. (5)

African-American Technician: I think the campaign was effective because it brought workers closer together. I wasn't there at the beginning of the plant, but when the management started getting away from the people, the plant started going down hill and there are so many shifts. . . . When the union came in and brought the workers together (some for the union and some against the union) but it brought us together to talk, we all learned about each other. 'Cause, you see, the company is twice the size of what it was then. Us getting together made the company open its eyes and say, "Hey, we're getting away from the people. We need to go back to the basics" (12)

White Technician: I think the campaign was real effective 'cause there were a few people like me who really wasn't sure, and they may have not all voted for the union, but they had a better understanding of what was really going on. And a lot of people in shipping and stuff weren't aware that we were having problems in production and we weren't aware of some of the problems they were having in shipping. So the campaign really helped pull all of us together better and it made people more informed and that's what made us union. (10)

African-American Technician: You know what really made the campaign successful was the way the union utilized the people. Because most of the campaign was done by the people, by the workers. The union would give us a general idea of what they wanted to do and then they would leave it up to whoever volunteered to make up the pamphlet or whatever. We could express ourselves any way and that's what made it successful. Workers basically had control over what was being said. It wasn't like the guys that were organizing the union came out there and said, "We're going to put this in the newsletter or put this in the cartoon." We had a choice. And being together really helped us get to know each other for the first time. (3)

Workers reasoned that they attained union success because of their ability to build a united community guided by employee action.

Throughout the descriptions of the campaign, workers used language that illustrated their sense of efficacy and their related perception of the "union as the workers." For instance, employees made comments such as "The campaign was great because it showed *us* what *we* can do together" and "What *we* really learned is that there has to be two-way communication. *We're* valuable to the company too and that is an important lesson to learn." The usage of the word "we" rather than "they" throughout workers' comments conveys that GM employees felt efficacious during the organizing campaign.

The ideology that the organizers fostered among GM workers was somewhat similar to the ideology established by the organizers at BGS. Workers were taught to view the union in instrumental terms. They asked themselves, "Is the union beneficial?" Yet, rather than ask how the union would help "me," employees from the clothing workers campaign asked how the union would serve "us." Seventy percent of the GM workers learned during the campaign that only a united group could implement change at the plant. As the following technicians explained:

> *African-American Worker:* The company tried to pull us apart, and you just need to be intelligent as to what's going on. You cannot be selfish about it either. You can't think, how will it guarantee me personally, but what can it guarantee us as a group. Because we're only as strong as united we are. (2)

> *White Worker:* I learned that workers have rights, they don't have to take everything that's dished out to them. If people stick together they can get more out of a group than they can out of being solo. You have more chance of achieving what you want. (8)

> *White Worker:* Everybody has to join the union because if we have the majority of all the employees then the working conditions would be a lot better. If we were all together, then they wouldn't be able to do anything without all of us. How are they going to run that place without us? (5)

The organizers conveyed to GM workers a "group" ideology, the idea that "the union is only as strong as its people." This concept of unionism facilitated a sense of community among employees. As one white technician admitted about the newly gained unity:

> When I say "they" I'm talking about the union. It's hard to start saying "us" because it's always just been "me." Like I said, it's all so new to me, the whole concept of a union, being together as a group rather than alone. It's new to most of us. (10)

Workers at GM did not view the union in radical terms. They did not see it as a vehicle to overthrow capitalism. However, organizers fostered a belief that, by working together, employees could get what they wanted from the company; through a shared "voice" they could have more say. Indeed, of the thirteen union workers with whom I spoke who had no prior union history, twelve said that the purpose of unions was to give the employee more "voice." On the other hand, the four union people with union experience said that the purpose of unions was to provide the worker protection. Clearly, the ideology organizers nourished during this specific campaign about unions involved employee "voice" through group action.

Conclusion

The one similarity both BGS and GM employees shared is that they regarded the union mainly in instrumental terms. However, BGS workers evaluated the union based on how they could benefit individually, while the employees at GM felt that nothing would be gained from the union unless all workers were united. These different ideologies, individualism on one hand and solidarity on the other, emerged directly from workers' experiences during the campaigns. At BGS, organizers "sold" workers the idea that the union could benefit them personally. They encouraged each employee to do a simple cost-benefit analysis to determine whether or not to sign a card. Were higher wages, job security, and retirement benefits worth union dues? Employees of BGS developed a "union as business" framework as a result. They felt that the union, like a business, employed "pushy salesmen" who did not inform them about the whole product. Ultimately, the business aspect of the union dissatisfied workers and made them feel inefficacious.

Active, prounion employees at GM felt positive about their experiences during the organizing campaign. After organizers conveyed that the campaign would only be successful given their input, workers pressured each other to participate. Through their collective efforts, workers gained a sense of community, a sense that fostered a "union as workers" framework. Workers reasoned that participation was necessary if they wanted the union at GM. As a result of the campaign's success, workers developed a deep sense of efficacy; they believed that what made the campaign successful was the solidarity and activism among the workforce. In the next chapter, I discuss the way self-efficacy (or lack thereof) explains activism after the campaigns end.

6

The Contract Period and Beyond: Activism and Efficacy Among Workers

Introduction

Winning union recognition does not ensure that workers will achieve union representation. A contract must first be negotiated. The negotiation period can be lengthy and difficult; both company and union representatives want a document that benefits them. Furthermore, with businesses now actively trying to avoid unions, companies sometimes use the ambiguous legal regulation, "bargaining in good faith," to evade ever settling upon a contract. The more time that passes from the election date, the less likely it is that a contract is going to be accepted and signed, and the more likely it is that employees will act out in frustration by decertifying a union (Freeman 1985). During contract negotiations, then, unions must sometimes strategize against business resistance with much the same resources and vigor that they utilized during the campaigns.

At Bob's Grocery Stores (BGS) and Geofelt Manufacturing (GM), however, the contract periods passed without much excitement or fanfare. Through quiet negotiations, BGS and the union decided upon a contract only six weeks after union recognition. Union officials felt justified in excluding BGS workers from the negotiation process because the union was primarily interested in establishing a strong contract standard for the industry. Employees of BGS were disappointed about being excluded. However, they had little expectation that contract negotiations would be organized differently from the campaign itself. For the most part, they passively accepted their exclusion.

Workers at GM, on the other hand, began the contract period with high expectations that they would control the negotiations and became frustrated when the participatory democratic structure of the campaign deteriorated. The union could not justify leaving an organizer during the six months it took to negotiate a contract at the small plant. Instead, a union negotiator flew into town occasionally to meet with company officials. In the end, the negotiator settled upon a contract quickly, conducting a vote with less than half of the members present. Workers at GM were bitter and disappointed that they were excluded from the process. Indeed, five workers tried to begin a decertification campaign after the contract was signed.

Although both the grocery and clothing workers' unions excluded workers from contract negotiations, BGS and GM employees reacted differently to their exclusion: GM workers acted out, BGS workers remained quiescent. I explain these different responses through contextualizing workers' experiences during the campaigns. The frameworks employees developed, the efficacy they gained, and the skills they acquired help clarify the quantity and quality of action workers took after their campaigns ended.

I begin the chapter describing the contract negotiation periods at BGS and GM. I am interested in how organizing strategies diffuse or constrain worker activism in different settings and across time. Thus, I describe how BGS and GM workers reacted to their exclusion from the negotiation process in two distinct time periods, during the contract period and three to five months after the contract was ratified.

The Contract Period

Bob's Grocery Stores

After BGS recognized the union in November 1992, contract negotiations between the two parties began. The local president and other officials from the regional office took control during the negotiating process. The company was represented by its officials and lawyers. Employees of BGS, in their own words, were just ''stuck in the middle'' during the process, without knowledge of what the company or the union was doing. There were three types of union meetings with employees during the contract negotiation period: (1) pizza parties to encourage workers to join the union, (2) small meetings with a select group of workers to relay what the union was doing, and (3) companywide meetings to inform workers about the negotiated contract. None of the meetings were designed to involve BGS employees in the contract process. Indeed, the main function of the meetings was to convince workers that joining the union would be beneficial for them.

When workers tried to become active without the permission of the organizers, union officials took control of the activism and tried to restrain future uninvited participation. For example, I attended one meeting with two organizers, Pete and Tony, that was supposed to represent the second type of meeting, where a select group of workers met with organizers. However, when we arrived at the restaurant, twenty-two BGS employees were there. Pete and Tony were very upset because they perceived that the workers were antiunion. During the course of the meeting, workers vented their anger towards the union and certain co-workers. Pete and Tony regulated the conflict by claiming to be in "control" of the issues. I include a large section of my notes to illustrate two points: (1) organizers tried to control who participated during the contract process and how, and (2) organizers did not use the meetings to involve workers in the process.

> At the meeting, which took place at a pizza place next door to BGS, twenty-two people showed up at various times. Half were women; all of them were white. Pete was not happy that the meeting was so large. We sat at a long table. Pete sat at one end and Tony was at the other. I sat near Tony. People wanted to know what the contract would say. Pete said that they weren't sure at this point what the contract would say, but they were going for industry standards: that is, pension, insurance, minimum hours. One woman at the end of the table where I sat began an argument with Tony. She said that she was mad at the union because some organizers had lied to them and told them to sign a card without explaining it to them. Another woman sitting near her said, "Yeah, one woman from the union approached me and she was so rude when I wouldn't sign a card, but she wouldn't explain it to me." The first woman said that, now that the union was here, there was friction between workers. She was mad because everything was peaceful until the union came, but now people were screaming in her face if she asked any questions. She kept saying that she wanted to know the truth, but when Tony spoke, she interrupted, saying that she wanted the friction to end. Tony said that any time she wanted to set up a meeting with him and her friends, he'd be there.
>   The two women also said that they were concerned about their hours.

If the union had a minimum-hour clause of twenty hours, then some people were going to be laid off because not everyone could have twenty hours. They said that, in the summer, business was dead and they'd rather have six hours than none. Tony said that the contract was ultimately up to the workers, who could say "no" if they didn't want it. Tony said, "The decision is yours, ultimately, because the contract is for you." Pete said the same thing.

The first woman said that there were some workers who would get in your face and she wouldn't take it. She said, "No one approached me about the union." A woman two seats down said, "That's because we all thought you would run and tell [the manager] what we said to you." The first woman said, "See what I mean? What are you going to do about people like that?" Tony said, "But people like that aren't in charge, we are." The first lady said, "I know you're in charge and she can't do any-thing, but when people have that attitude, it turns me off." Tony told the ladies that they would have their choice of shop stewards. People began leaving at 5:30. I heard two woman talking as they left. One of them said, "They didn't tell us anything. It's all tentative. They don't even know anything." At six, the meeting wrapped up. There were two women left and two men. Pete shook the hands of the two men and said we had to go. I followed Pete out. He said, "I'm so mad at Tony, I can't see straight. This is what you call a setup." When Tony got out, Pete asked, "What were all those anti's doing there?" Tony said, "I don't know. I know one thing, I'm not going back there again. The next time they'll see me is at the ratification meeting." Pete said, "You know the problem? It's the man-ager. He's gotta go and I'm going to make sure of it, even if I have to move closer to this store so I can see him every day." Tony said, "I think something good came out of it, though."

Pete asked me if he made a fool of himself at the meeting. I said that I couldn't really hear what he was talking about because I was listening to Tony. I said that I didn't understand how the meeting went bad because I have nothing to compare it to. He said, "Go to the meeting at 7:00—you'll have something to compare it to then. You'll see how things are supposed to go. The people are handpicked and there'll be respect and courtesy." Pete said there was no way they were going to elect stewards there if someone like the produce manager could get it. He said he was going to appoint them himself.

During the course of the meeting, workers conveyed to organizers that they were nervous that the contract would cause layoffs and divisions within the workplace. Organizers placated the fears by promising that the workers controlled the contract outcome. Tony said, "The decision is yours." However, BGS employees were never allowed a formal vote on the contract. Furthermore, after the meeting was over, Pete admitted to me that the union would actually take more control over the union process, not less, by appointing union stewards. The meet-ings, then, were not designed to include workers in the contract. Instead, the various types of meetings, including the one described above, were intended to control the type of information workers received and the way they received it.

Ultimately, the goal for the union was to devise an above-industry-level contract so the other local stores would have a standard to work towards after their contracts expired; the goal was not to include BGS workers in the negotiation process. Involving employees, according to one organizer, "just complicates the process because everybody has their own thing they're interested in." (7)

In the end, the union felt they achieved an excellent contract for BGS workers. They attained a raise for grocery workers, established retirement benefits for employees, and established a provision called time maximization, a policy that forced BGS to use mostly full-time instead of part-time help. When the contract was agreed upon by the union and the company in December, there was not an election. Several union meetings occurred so that the contract could be explained to all BGS employees, and there was even a pseudovote when the president asked all those who were for the contract to raise their hands. However, the contract had already been signed and authorized by officials.

Geofelt Manufacturing

The successful union campaign at GM took only six weeks. However, contract negotiations extended over six months. The union was voted in the spring of 1993 and the contract was not attained until November of that year. Employees of GM were confused why a protracted contract period was necessary. A breakdown in participatory democracy exacerbated workers' confusion.

The union attempted to design a participatory democratic structure at the beginning of the contract process. A workers' committee, consisting of five employees elected by democratic procedures, was present during all the contract meetings with the company.[1] Yet, even with this participatory structure, three members of the committee and most workers claimed they had no opportunity to become active during the negotiation process. Two aspects of the contract period prevented workers from becoming active participants. First, workers had little interaction with the contract negotiator. No representative of the union was consistently present for the workers during the negotiations. The clothing workers' union commonly conducts contract negotiations in the same fashion as the organizing campaign. Organizers are present for the duration of negotiations to keep employees informed and to bolster morale during the potentially lengthy time period. Given the small size of the GM plant, however, the union did not have the resources to keep an organizer present during the negotiations. One veteran organizer apologized for having to consider the costs and benefits of keeping a paid staff at the campaign site. He explained:

> It's hard for us to dole out resources to a plant of only fifty people, which is a shame because workers in a small unit have the right to a union just like any other. It may seem callous, but it is the cost-benefit here that is the reality. Unions are not rich organizations. We operate on our members' dues so we have to look practically. Like with Geofelt, a plant with seventy-five people, we will not benefit from those dues because that means that a rep will spend time there.

The union rationally made the choice not to leave a union representative; the cost was not justified with such a small plant. However, the failure of the union to make a representative available for GM employees contributed to the breakdown in participatory democracy. During the campaign, interactions with organizers had been considered crucial for two reasons: the organizer disseminated information from one group of employees to another and educated workers about the function of unions and how to win the election. Shared information and education abetted the attempt of GM employees to unite. Without a full-time union representative present during the contract negotiations, however, GM employees were without a fundamental source of continuous information and education, and without external stimulation to coalesce.

Furthermore, many workers claimed that they did not have time to interact with the representative even when he was present. The union contract negotiator appeared at the plant only during the days when meetings with the company were scheduled and left soon after the meetings ended. Thus, the negotiator's short and irregular visits prevented workers from having input during the negotiation period.

Another issue that prevented activism among most of the employees was that the union did not provide workers with information and education about the contract process. The union promised training for the workers' committee so they would have the skills for negotiating a contract. However, the union never provided the training. As a result, three members of the committee admitted that they felt lost during the contract meetings because they did not understand the process nor the technical and legalistic jargon batted back and forth. One white member of the negotiating committee said:

> I started bringing up issues towards the end of the negotiations and [the negotiator] said, "Well, ya'll should have brought it up at the first." I was thinking, "I just thought of it. I'm not geared or equipped to handle this." I still don't agree with the way it was conducted. (5)

Furthermore, many workers not on the negotiating committee had even less information about the contract process. The majority of employees assumed that their fellow workers on the committee understood what was happening during the negotiations and simply chose not to reveal everything to them. Even when the negotiation committee admitted that they, too, were being excluded from the process, some employees did not believe them. One white worker questioned:

> How could they not know what was going on? They were sitting right there! (11)

Thus, communication broke down not only between the union and the negotiating committee, but also between the workers on the negotiating committee and the rank and file.

Many employees who complained about the contract period contrasted it to the ease of information, communication, and decision-making during the organizing campaign. Two African-American technicians claimed:

> After the campaign, the union was dragging their feet, the company was dragging their feet and it took them a while to get to the table and negotiate the contract. And it drug on, drug on and on, and after a while you become disinterested. You're not as motivated as you were and things like that. There were no meetings, and they just got disenchanted by the whole thing. Especially because of the way the campaign was, you know, so active and all. We just didn't know what to do and the union just seemed like they left us. We should have started meetings to get people motivated. Give a barbecue again. Come together and talk and do it that way. (2)

> They gave us a big pause after the election. We didn't hear for a while and people started asking questions. People on the negotiating team weren't relaying messages very well. They didn't tell us what was going on. The lack of communication was the biggest problem. Like I said, before the election we were meeting [the organizer] all the time and communication was always open. We had someone on hand to talk to us and teach us how to get things done. But all of a sudden everything stopped. (7)

What employees missed during the contract period was the ease of communication that they considered essential for their high morale and activism during the campaign.

Some workers further complained that when they did have the opportunity to speak with the union negotiator, he ignored their concerns. The African-American technician mentioned above who discussed the ''big pause'' explained:

> When they were doing the contract we told them the times that were best for us. But they just came when they had a chance. They scheduled meetings on their time, not ours. When they came in to help do the contract, the negotiator starts telling us what he thought we needed. That really heated people up. When he started telling us what we needed, people got mad and morale really dropped. (7).

The union negotiator denied that he failed to listen to people's concerns. However, he indicated that some of the workers' issues were untenable, and thus he could not bring them up with management. He said:

> Now when we left Geofelt I think there were a number of workers who were unsatisfied with the economic settlement, especially the wage settlement. What I promised those workers, what our committee promised those workers at the end of negotiations, was come back in three years and look at the difference in your pay. Because just by giving them an across-the-board raise, you can only do certain things. The important thing at Geofelt was that people get evaluated fairly, and accurately, and in a timely way because their real raises were by moving up the steps in the evaluation chain.

Even if the negotiator honestly explained why he chose to pursue bargaining for prompt evaluations rather than for higher across-the-board raises, he still only provided these explanations after he negotiated with the company rather than before. The conflict between the negotiator and workers existed, then, because GM employees were excluded from the process of negotiation.

After six months of negotiations, the union and company finally agreed upon a contract on a November day. The negotiator felt very pleased with the outcome of the negotiations. The racist manager was fired, favoritism was reduced by replacing managerial evaluators with peer evaluators, and workers were given more say in the production line by supplanting assistant supervisors (not members of the bargaining unit) with lead technicians (members of the bargaining unit). Employees of GM were called at home and told to come and vote on the contract that night or the next day until noon. Not all union members, however, could be reached by phone.

Due to misinformation, many workers thought the contract could not be accepted without the vote of every union member; they were dismayed to learn that the union contract had been accepted with a vote consisting of less than half the eligible workforce. One African-American technician described the problem at length:

> The negotiation process, nobody was kept informed and I think you really need to keep your people informed of what's going on. 'Cause if you don't keep people informed, people will lose touch and they feel like, "Hey, they got my vote and now they're just going to forget about me." They didn't keep us informed like they should have. Even when it come contract vote time. You saw some of that by the lack of turnout for the vote on the contract.
>
> *Interviewer: What do you mean?*
> Well, the guys hadn't been told, and next thing you know, we're voting on the contract. They hadn't heard a lot of what was going on. We just got a briefing that morning, you know, and it's like, we had guys on our shift that didn't even vote for it.
>
> *Interviewer: Why didn't they keep people more informed?*
> I don't know. That's what I haven't got an answer for. Each shift had a negotiating committee member. I think they did good. I mean most of the guys had never been involved with anything like this. I think that's a point where an organizer or a local representative needs to say, "Hey, we need to do things this way, we need to keep people informed. I know you've never been in a union. I know you ain't never done this before, but we need to keep people informed." There should have been meetings for each shift so the representative could keep people informed about what they were trying to do and ask people what do you all think of it. I mean, don't wait until the last minute and just say, "Well, this is what we've done." And that's the way to keep people motivated too, by keeping them informed. If you keep people more informed and let them have their say, they feel more part of the process. (13)

The formal structure of the contract period embodied principles of inclusion: workers democratically voted upon a workers' committee and then on the negotiated contract. However, the informal process of negotiation excluded worker activism. Committee members often felt lost during the contract procedure and, as a result, did not competently educate the rest of the rank and file. Furthermore, the contract vote was done in such haste that not all workers had the opportunity to vote. In the end, the contract period involved the theory of participatory democracy but not its practice.

Activism and Self-Efficacy During the Contract Period

Bob's Grocery Stores

The contract process at BGS passed in much the same way as the campaign. The union did encourage activism more during the contract period so that organizers could convince workers to join the union. Yet, of the thirty workers with whom I spoke, all agreed that the union controlled the contract outcome. The most obvious evidence for workers was that the union did not provide a formal vote to decide upon the contract. Although the union did conduct meetings, the meetings simply described what had already been agreed upon by the union and management. Two BGS employees explained:

> *Union, Female Cashier:* When I got home from the meeting I realized that the hand-raising didn't mean anything at all. Not only was it not legal, but it didn't matter how many hands were raised because they weren't really counted. Then they told us the contract had already been passed. We might as well not have had that meeting at all.
>
> *Interviewer: How did you feel about that?*
> I just think the contract was agreed upon much more by BGS management than it was agreed upon by BGS employees. (26)
>
> *Union, Male Stocker:* I went to the contract meeting. They had it all printed out and we went over it page by page. The thing I didn't like is this big guy was standing at the door and he said, "Welcome, brother." And I thought, "Hey, I'm not your brother, leave me alone." They were trying to shake my hand and I didn't appreciate that. See, I wasn't too thrilled to join the union. I was walking in wondering whether to join, and here's this guy . . . there was a lot of excitement. You could see it. People were excited . . . and the union people put a lot of time in to getting Bob's union, and they were real excited about it. Maybe that was part of the thing, calling you brother, making you feel at home and part of it. I myself didn't appreciate it. Besides, everything was already printed out for the contract so they obviously weren't looking for our feedback. (4)

All BGS employees agreed that the actions by the union created the contract; workers were simply supposed to decide whether or not the contract benefited them. As a result, workers admitted to having little sense of efficacy.

When workers related their feelings about the contract, they expressed a clear sense of powerlessness. Fifty percent of the workers I interviewed said that during the contract negotiations they either felt "stuck in the middle" or like "peons." The following workers illustrate:

Union Photo/Sound Clerk: The contract was just between management and the union people. Us peons don't count. That's my theory, we peons don't count. But we're smarter than managers.

Interviewer: How could you be counted more?
They should listen to us instead of only the people higher up. They don't work, we do.

Interviewer: Could unions be a way for management to listen to you more?
They are supposed to, I guess. But they don't. Employees know more. They know what's going on the floor more than managers. And if union reps would listen to the employees more than they would listen to the managers, it would be a better working place. That's always been my theory. Employees know more than managers do and union people need to talk to the employees to find out how to make the workplace better.

Interviewer: If you went to the union, do you think they would listen to you?
Probably not. I don't know, maybe they would listen, but nothing would get done. (15)

Union Stocker: During the contract, management would be sitting at the same table as you after the union left and they'd say, ''Stick union in the back.'' And the union would do the same. We were caught in the middle, kind of like, holy cow. You have no control. (5)

Workers from BGS felt that the contract was just between the union and management, leaving them without control.

Besides feeling little efficacy, BGS employees were disappointed with several of the contract outcomes. First, half of the workers mentioned that the contract was just an amalgamation of other existing grocery-store contracts and had nothing specific about BGS's unique situation as both grocery and general merchandise store. One union male scanning coordinator stated:

The union says they work for the employee, so I think our contract should be different from Food-for-Cheap. It's just going to bother me forever that they didn't do the leg work to find out about us because Bob's is different. We need to be represented as a company but because our union is too busy to give us what we need. . . . The union contract is written for the grocery side and they just added us. I don't think the people from the union understood what Bob's structure is. I think they just said, ''Here's the contract we have for the other grocery stores, sign this.'' And I think that's pretty sad. It doesn't give me a lot of confidence in this union. (1)

The second complaint voiced by 60 percent of the interviewed employees had to do with the provision called ''time maximization.'' Time maximization forced BGS to schedule most workers for forty hours over six days during the work week. In theory, this provision is positive in that it compels an industry moving towards part-time workers to rely on full-time workers instead. However, BGS employees were upset by time maximization because, as the workers from the pizza meeting suspected, it led to the layoff of five hundred workers. Also, some workers who were attracted to the job because of part-time work could no longer keep their flexible hours. One female cashier explained:

> A lot of the girls didn't want to work six days a week. They didn't want to work forty hours, they had children to take care of. But they were told that either you maximize your hours or go down to the bottom of the seniority list. (6)

Hence, while the union officials were excited that they were able to provide BGS workers with more benefits than employees from other chains received, the workers from BGS were not equally satisfied. Once again, the exclusion from the union process, this time during the contract negotiation, made workers feel disappointed in the union.

Employees at BGS claimed that their dissatisfaction during the contract negotiations stemmed from the problematic contract provisions and not from their being excluded from control over the process. However, they still expressed a strong desire for "voice" in the union. This contradiction makes sense when we consider the "union as business" framework. The longing for employee "voice" existed because workers believed that only by having better communication with union officials could they be assured of getting what they paid for. The general feeling was expressed by one nonunion Latina cashier:

> You want answers and they don't have them or they just, you know, blow you off. So that's what we get from them. I mean nobody's going to want to join if they're going to blow them off like that. I mean you're paying your money—you expect something to be done. (13)

The exclusion of employee voice was most glaring in the lack of say workers had in what the union contract stated. Employees felt that, since they were paying the union to represent their needs, they had a right to have a say in the contract. Two employees claimed:

> *Nonunion, Male Cashier:* I may be wrong, but as far as I know, there were no employees involved whatsoever in the contract. There were a few people from each store that became the shop foremen, but as far as the negotiations, no, there were no employees involved.
> *Interviewer: Did you think there would be?*
> Well, they're negotiating your contract, so you think that you would be

> involved in it, since it's your contract. If I were an employee that were voting for it, I'd feel deceived because they did things without my knowledge and bargained away a couple of fringe benefits. (16)
>
> *Union Photo/Sound Clerk:* The employees weren't involved in the contract, just the managers. I thought employees could get a little more involved and tell them their opinions about what could be done, but I haven't seen it happen yet.
>
> *Interviewer: How do you feel that more employees weren't more involved?* Well, if we have to pay union dues they should have the employees involved. The union's the one getting the money. We're paying them to help us and find out what our needs are. If employees can't get involved, what's the point of paying them? (15)

Employees wanted their actions to matter so that they would receive the goods they paid for, not so that they could make the union a worker-controlled organization. In the end, however, the desire for voice did not impel most workers towards activism.

Of the thirty workers I interviewed, 80 percent did not attend any of the meetings about contract negotiations. Two workers attended a pizza party and four went to a store-wide meeting. However, one worker narrated a story of unsolicited activism. He and some coworkers collectively attempted to resist union control over the contract process. The union, male stocker explained:

> During the contract, the union told two girls that they could be union reps, but the employees didn't want these girls to be union reps. So the union asked these two girls to go to a meeting with them about the contract and the rest of us caught wind of it and thought, "Wait a minute." Fifteen or twenty of us went.[2] The union people were mad because they thought, "This is supposed to be just a little meeting." And we said, "We're from the same store so we have a right to know." And they said, "Well, we really don't know what's going on, the contract is still in limbo." They had no idea, they just beat the bull around for awhile. They were just smooth talkers. But anyway we ended up making a petition to try to get these two girls out and just in our store, and the union was kind of like, "What are you doing?" and we were like, "Well, we want the people in there who we want. We don't want these two girls." And they were like, "Well, we'll look at it, and see if we can honor this." But I don't really think it's up to them whether they honor it or not. If we decide we don't want them. . . . We need someone to communicate with these union guys because they're negotiating for us with management and the main office so we want someone we know and trust who can communicate what we want.
>
> *Interviewer: So what happened?*
> Well, they haven't changed it. And we haven't done anything else. (5)

Despite the union's control over the campaign and contract, this worker and his co-workers resisted the union's complete authority over the contract process. Workers legitimized their resistance within the "union as business" framework; they felt the union at least owed them a delegate from the store who would best represent their needs. However, when the union ignored their request, workers did not further protest. The stocker had not developed the cognitive or emotional skills during the campaign to think his actions could make a difference within the union. Instead, he said that, as long as he received his pension, he would not cause any other problems:

> I don't like it. But then again, if they give me a pension, then I'll like them. (5)

The impotency BGS workers admitted feeling after the union entered the workplace translated into an apathy regarding what the union contract could and did provide for the employees. Given that contractualism embodies the relationship the union has with the company, workers are incapable, at the most fundamental level, of becoming active in the union without knowledge of what the contract says. When I asked BGS workers about the contract, many answered that they were not sure what it entailed. Indeed, 50 percent said that they had not received a copy of the contract. One woman who recently was diagnosed with cancer and joined the union for fear of losing her job stated:

> If you ask me about the contract, I have to say I don't know because I haven't seen it. They never sent me a copy of it. You have to go to the union to get a copy and I don't know if I care for one. (6)

Thirteen percent admitted that they were not sure if they had received the contract. As this cashier, whose father was a member of the union in the meat department at BGS, expressed:

> I don't know if I have a copy of the contract. Maybe that's in the big packet that they give you. There's a lot of papers but I didn't read it all. I wasn't really that interested. (23)

Another 13 percent said that they had received the contract but had not read it. One male stocker who felt very bitter about the layoffs admitted:

> I have a copy of the contract and I thumbed through it, but I'm not interested, I'm just not interested. (7)

In all, 76 percent of the workers interviewed claimed that they had little concern about the contents of the union contract.

During the campaign, workers learned that their actions were immaterial in establishing a union. This lesson was replicated during the contract period. Employees had no interest in the contract because they felt that they had no control over the contract; the union and company would do what they wanted regardless of the workers. Without sufficient motivation to find out the contents of the contract, workers are unlikely to assert their rights with the company or the union.

Geofelt Manufacturing

When I asked GM employees what made the organizing campaign successful, they answered like this white technician:

> It was the workers because we are the union and we had taken so much. It was time to stand up and all help together. (4)

However, people's experiences with the contract period were quite different. Seventy percent of the union workers stated, in stark contrast to the campaign, that the union representative controlled the contract negotiations. One white technician explained:

> When the organizers left and we got turned over to the local, it seemed like we weren't getting the inflow of information we once were. I think it's one of the shortcomings of the union. And I think that's why our contract wasn't that great. When the inflow of information quit, people started turning against the union. Even though you had people vote for it, you start losing their support. It's easier to run through a brick wall when you see some bricks missing than it is to run through one when they're all there. And I think management saw that, saw the position of weakness among the workers and it was weak.
> *Interviewer: Why did the information stop?*
> I don't know. You're dealing with the same union, but you're dealing with different people during the campaign than the contract. And you don't know if it was the people or a lack of concern. 'Cause they could say, well, we've been voted in now and so we've got it here and we don't need to give these people information anymore. You know it's one of the two but you don't know which one to blame things on. (13)

Workers attributed the lessening of union support to the lack of information, whatever its cause.

Two workers used the same imagery to describe their disappointment in the transformation of control: they said the campaign and contract periods were as different as "day and night":

> *White Technician:* I feel like we were screwed by the company and the union representatives during the contract talks. If they were truly concerned and interested, they would have asked questions. They would not have waited for our input, they would have come looking for it. And while they looked for some input, they didn't look for it hard enough. It was totally different than the campaign. It was the difference between day and night. (5)
>
> *African-American Technician:* I was a firm believer that you are the union. You know, that's what they told us in the campaign, "You are the one that makes the decisions." But it wasn't like that with this union during the contract. I don't know. It was just like day and night. (16)

Employees of GM developed a "union as workers" framework during the campaign; a belief that "we" are the union. When the union organized contract negotiations around union-control rather than worker-control, employees felt dissatisfied. Workers began to ask themselves, who is the union if it is not the employees? The "union as business" analogy, which none of the workers invoked to describe the campaign, emerged among three workers when they described the contract period. One African-American technician claimed:

> I haven't been in this particular union before, but ah, there was a business side to them wanting the contract, ratified and signed as quick as possible. (2)

Workers, then, began to question their ownership of the union during contract negotiations.

The breakdown in the participatory democratic structure created several problems besides dissatisfaction. First, twenty-five percent of the GM employees were angered because the union failed to honor its promise to provide two types of education classes for the employees: one for workers on the negotiating committee about how to negotiate a contract and the other for the new officers of the union about the structure and organization of unions. Two technicians described the problem:

> *White Technician:* We don't really know how to be union. That's why I think that the union needs to come back in and train us. We was told during the election process that they was going to train the shop stewards. They had a workshop they were going to send the shop steward to, the officers too, and everything. But they haven't. After a while, you get disgusted and want to pull out from it.

Interviewer: Are you disgusted?
Well, not so much disgusted. Frustrated would be a better term. (19)

African-American Technician: For the contract, we should have gotten together with people from the union and went over this thing, studied things
for a couple of weeks and then come back and try to ratify this contract.
It was more or less pushed down our throat. And training, we still need to
be trained. Man can't be president of this union if he never been president
before unless he's had training. He don't know what to do. We need training and education and we need someone to come in and do it for us. I
know we don't have a big staff at our union office. But we need someone
to train us about how to be more efficient and how to best use the contract.
'Cause we don't understand it right now. (2)

During the campaign, organizers promised GM workers that classes
would provide them with the necessary education to maintain their
solidarity and activism after the campaign ended. Workers clearly understood that they needed different skills to negotiate a contract and
maintain a union than to carry on a campaign. Therefore, they saw
the union's promise of education as essential for their strength as a
local. When the union failed to honor its promise, then, GM employees felt angry and frustrated.

A second problem that occurred during the contract period was that
divisions among workers arose. The company's attempt to divide and
conquer during the campaign had been unsuccessful: the only "division" that employees discussed during the campaign was between
pro- and antiunion employees. Ironically, only after the company refrained from trying to harm solidarity did strife among union
employees emerge. Thirty percent of the workers I interviewed mentioned that the contract period created divisions among the union people. Solidarity broke down along racial lines: two white employees
complained that they were suspicious because the majority of members on the negotiating committee were black. It also broke down
along departmental lines: one African-American worker said that the
technicians on the committee did not take into account any other department except their own during the negotiations. Finally, solidarity
broke down along formal union position lines: three employees (two
African-American and one white) admitted that they did not believe
that their co-workers on the negotiating committee had the interest of
the workers at heart during negotiations. One African-American technician discussed to what he attributed the discordance:

They just never posted any negotiating meetings. Really, we . . . it was real
odd. It's like they was keeping everything from the people. It was very

bizarre to me because of the campaign. We always had meetings. The workers had to agree on everything, not just three or four negotiating workers. We talked about them having meetings, but we never had any.
Interviewer: So did you bring it up to someone?
Yeah, as a matter of fact, we would ask the negotiators, you know, are we going to have a meeting on this? It's like, there's going to be a meeting at a later date. I was telling everyone, "We still gotta stay together. We still got to, we need this union." And the campaign was beautiful, like a family. And it turned sour. I think things started turning sour when we voted in these committee people. Jim was not elected. Jeff was not elected. You know, little things like that was starting people to get into their own little groups in the corners and tables and whispering about who voted for who and . . . stuff like that. (16)

During the contracts, workers failed to trust each other. Some employees accused each other of being self-interested, and these accusations caused factions. Ultimately, without clear communication, GM workers were unable to perpetuate the momentum of solidarity established during the campaign.

I want to also make clear that five union employees felt very satisfied with the contract process.[3] Four of these employees were either on the negotiating committee or "good" friends with someone on the committee. The satisfied employees denied the charges about the breakdown in participatory democracy. They argued that information, communication, and decision-making were as free-flowing as previously. One white technician claimed:

I really feel good about the contract because we had some say. The reason I say this is because the majority of the issues were an altogether thing. There wasn't anything in the contract that was individualized. So I felt we were involved in it even though there were only five people on the negotiating committee. Since we were kept up to date, we felt a part of it. If everyone was informed like we were, they would probably feel part of it too. So I thought the contract was handled real well. (10)

Satisfied union workers attributed their positive feelings to how the negotiation committee members kept them informed about the negotiation process. Problems arose, however, because not everyone felt as informed as these five felt.

Despite anger with the way the contract was handled, 60 percent of the employees I interviewed felt that their sense of efficacy within the workplace was enhanced directly after the campaign. One white technician said:

I have a lot of frustrations towards the union. The communication flow from the negotiation committee was . . . it wasn't up to speed I don't think.

> But I have some gratitude towards the union, 'cause there was some things
> that needed to be addressed and changed, and I mean right after the cam-
> paign things changed. (14)

Workers at GM said that the campaign forced supervisors to listen to employees, and that their new "voice" gave them more control at work:

> *African-American Technician:* Because with the union, since we had the
> campaign, the attitude of the company, they listen more.
> *Interviewer: That's interesting. Why?*
> Because we had the union, we got together. Before, it was like do it my
> way or we don't do it any way at all. That has changed a great deal. And
> that's for the whole plant, not just the supervisors, management and all.
> *Interviewer: Why do you think they listen more since the campaign?*
> I think it's because they realize the concept that the union brought. It's
> gotta be a two-way street, two-way communication. Like, it's not that it's
> going to be your way and your way only. You gotta listen to both sides.
> This guy, even though he's a technician, his idea might be just as good as
> yours. I think they realize that concept now. I really do. (2)

The enhanced self-efficacy that workers described centered around having more control over the workplace. Employees of GM felt that supervisors finally began recognizing the valuable knowledge that workers possessed.

The newly developed self-efficacy translated into increased work-place activism for many GM employees. First, 10 percent of the employees I interviewed stated that they were now willing to defend each other inside the workplace. One African-American employee, for example, narrated a story of how he accused his supervisor of racial discrimination when the supervisor "wrote up" only an African-American worker for failing to co-write a report rather than writing up all four workers, three of them white, who were responsible for the report. He said:

> I went up and told the supervisor that that was discrimination and he said
> to let him do his job and I'd do mine. I said, well, fine, we'll see you later.
> So we're going to see him later. See, this was during the time we were
> trying to negotiate the contract, and by that time we knew what they could
> and couldn't do. (1)

Second, 20 percent of the employees (three white) said they brought suggestions to supervisors when they had not done so in the past. One white technician said:

That's one thing that has helped as far as the group because whereas people would sit back and just not say nothing because they was afraid they was going to get in trouble or be laughed at, now they don't mind coming to their shop steward or to, say, someone that was on the negotiating committee and asking questions or voicing a problem, whereas used to they were just mum about it.

Interviewer: Have you brought up anything that you wouldn't before?
Yeah, lots of stuff.

Interviewer: Like what?
Oh, anything, like we need our breaks now. Or I have to go home early. Or you might want to do the process this way instead of that way. Lots of stuff. I feel there is more chance to be open. (10)

Employees of GM mentioned many times that they felt more in control over the labor process after the campaign. One white employee succinctly summed it up:

They always wanted to think of ourselves as a team and now we finally are. (4)

One final example of newly inspired workplace activism occurred five months after the success of the GM organizing campaign when twelve black employees brought a racial discrimination suit against the company. The workers felt that the injustices they had experienced from the racist manager who had been fired must be redressed by the company. The employee who helped initiate the suit described the process as follows:

When [the organizers] were here and the campaign had just begun, they said that we had an open-and-shut case of discrimination. They pointed out that there were no blacks in any leadership positions, in the office or in the administrative side. The organizers didn't want to bring up a lawsuit during the campaign because they thought it would disturb it, but they promised to help afterwards. But they left and didn't do anything so I got some workers together and we went to a law firm, a place I had used on another occasion. (16)

Although the senior African-American employees admitted that they had experienced discrimination since the company's inception, they failed to bring a legal suit against GM until after the organizing campaign. Two skills, general and specific, helped workers collectively resist. First, workers realized they had to control the process in order to create change. They learned this "general" skill during the organizing campaign. While the organizers legitimized workers' beliefs that discrimination existed, they failed to fulfill their promise of bringing a suit against the company. Rather than allow the complaint to die, workers organized themselves using the solidarity they had established during the campaign. Second, one worker used the law firm that the employees had hired for another matter. His "specific" experiences with lawyers enabled him to obtain a lawyer and inform his co-workers about the legal process.

Workers at GM thus became active after the campaign by defending their co-workers, by taking suggestions to management, and by su-ing the company for discrimination. The efficacy workers developed during the campaign gave them the opportunity to create changes, and the cognitive skills they learned during the campaign helped trans-form the opportunity into reality.

Activism and Self-Efficacy After the Contract Period

Bob's Grocery Stores

Workers at BGS felt that their actions were immaterial in bringing the union into the workplace and, thus, most of the workforce viewed participation as either futile or unnecessary. Hence, the most common response of this group to unionization was inaction. As one white union cashier answered when I asked if she had talked to the union about a problem she was having:

> No. I think the union wants us just to pay dues and let them do things their way. (2)

Employees said that many of the problems they were experiencing at the workplace before the union, such as job instability, still persisted. This left workers feeling helpless and without recourse. As this non-union, Latina cashier admitted:

> There's not much else we can do since the union was supposed to make things better and didn't.
> *Interviewer: What do you mean that there's not much else you can do?*
> Well, if the union is supposed to exist to improve working conditions and if they worsen as a result, where else do you turn? Who do you trust? It's like you have no power, no say-so. (19)

The feeling of helplessness communicated by this worker and many others discouraged dissatisfied employees from making demands on either the union or the company.

One Latina cashier asserted that, worse than feeling powerless, she felt that the union took her "rights" away. This young woman was the most active worker I spoke with during the organizing campaign. She helped organizers get employees' names and phone numbers and convinced her co-workers to sign up. Her enthusiasm grew during the campaign when organizers helped her with a problem she was having. In the store location where she worked, employees' cars were sometimes vandalized and stolen. The union began a petition to persuade the company to provide a fence around the parking lot where employees parked. After the campaign, however, organizers left without pursuing the issue of the fence. Furthermore, the young woman felt that the union left without properly explaining the idea of unionism:

> When we signed those cards, they never told us about seniority, they should have explained things like that to us, but they didn't! They didn't explain anything to us. And our break. We used to get two breaks, now we only get one, and that's really hard. And a lot of employees feel this way, even ones that aren't union members. They didn't sign cards or anything, and they still have to go along with the union. They didn't have a choice either. And I called the union with a problem and they never called me back. You know, it's just the fact they didn't listen to my problems. They didn't work with me like the union said they would. Ever since then, I regret signing those union cards. I talked to a lot of other employees who feel like they signed their rights away. That's how we feel. We always talk to each other and we feel like we're their property, and it's true! They haven't even done anything about the parking lot. It's like they got what they wanted. Now the ones with seniority get to have whatever days they want. But what can we do? We signed the cards, we're union. We can't do much about it. That's how we feel. We signed our rights away because we signed those cards. That's why I would never go with the union again. And a lot of people feel the same way.
> *Interviewer: Have you done anything about the parking lot?*
> No, I'm not interested anymore.

Two issues made this young woman feel "owned" by the union. First, the union failed to educate workers about union policy and structure. She did not understand seniority and felt betrayed when her schedule was interrupted by its implementation. Five other employees I interviewed also complained about seniority and the division it caused among workers. Second, the union failed to return workers' calls, leaving employees with the feeling that they had no voice. Through her interactions with the union, then, the cashier learned that the union was controlled by union officials, not workers. Although she was enthusiastic about her activism during the campaign, eventually the young worker came to feel like property after the campaign ended.

Workers at BGS were not taught how to participate during the organizing campaign or during the contract period. As a result, workers took little action either to learn more about their rights under the newly formed contract or to try to change the situation at either the company or the union. One union cashier explain:

> *Interviewer: You were saying that you wish you could get more information. Could you talk with someone from the union about getting more information?*
> I suppose I could if I was really all that interested in it but right now I'm not. I think I'm like a lot of people that joined the union. We expected a lot. I don't know what we expected but we expected that they were going to do something for us. It's like we're disappointed that we didn't get it so we're just rolling along. Just rolling along. I don't know what we expected but we got nothing so we're just really going with the flow. It's like we're not trying to find out anything. Basically most of us are just doing nothing. (6)

Seventeen percent of the workers claimed that even though they were dissatisfied with the union, they had no recourse but to "grin and bear it":

> *Union Photo/Sound Clerk:* I'd like to tell them where they can take the union [laugh] and where to put it. I was really considering getting out of the union. It's just supposed to guarantee your job, but they still had layoffs, so that's not guaranteeing nothing.
> *Interviewer: When you say you were considering, what do you mean?*
> I've heard you can't get out of the union.
> *Interviewer: What do you mean?*
> Once you're in, you're sucked in, that's what I was told. (15)

In all, 70 percent of BGS employees said that they felt dissatisfied about the union contract and powerless to create change. Workers admitted that they were just "rolling along."

Workers at BGS asserted that their dissatisfaction had little to do with why they were not going to become active in the union. Fifty percent of the workers reasoned that they would not participate in the union because activism was not part of their role as a "union member." These two male employees explained:

> *Union Scanning Coordinator:* I don't need to become involved. We pay people to do that. We pay our leaders to find out what our needs are. We

pay organizers and the president to make sure our needs are taken care of. If they're doing their jobs, I shouldn't have to participate. (1)

Nonunion Cashier: Well, there's no place for you to be involved. It's not like a YMCA, where they need volunteers. It's a business like anything else, and there isn't any room for employee involvement. (16)

Assuming the logic of a business transaction, workers did not perceive that participation was part of their role in the exchange relationship. Rather, it was the responsibility of the union officials to maintain the union. In exchange, the workers would pay dues. A comparison with the expectations of a buyer in a different type of exchange relationship is illustrative. For example, an accident lawyer promises to do all the necessary work for a client in exchange for a percentage of the settlement after the case is tried and won in court. If the lawyer asked a potential client to help out with the case, the client would likely feel that the transaction was unfair. Similarly, most BGS workers believed that asking them to participate was unfair given the "union as business" framework they had developed during the organizing campaign. For them, employee participation was a negative characteristic of the union, a sign that the union was not doing its job.

Even when workers decided to participate in the union, they did so within the "union as business" ideology. For instance, one shop steward relayed a story to me about the time he filed a grievance for a co-worker:

There was an incident with our store manager so I called the union and the rep couldn't get to the store so he told me to write down the grievance. I didn't file the grievance because it was about my department manager. The rep said he'd talk to him and get back to us and I haven't heard from him. That's the stuff that really bugs me. Now, I don't know if he ever did talk to him. I don't know whether or not it got blown off, I don't know if the grievance ever got filed. They never contacted us. That stuff is really, is really . . . it kind of gets you after a while. When you feel like you're paying your money out, the least they can do is take care of you. But I always try to see two sides to everything, and I'm sure they're understaffed and they only have so many reps for all the stores, but that doesn't make it right. I'm not trying to justify it. (20)

The shop steward participated by helping his co-worker contact the union about a grievance. However, when the union did not respond, the employee did not pursue the issue. Rather, he became angry that the bargain he made was not being honored; he was paying his dues, but he was not receiving union benefits.

The "business transaction" framework permeated every type of relationship workers had with the union, from feelings of satisfaction and efficacy to decisions to participate. Indeed, after the union was accepted by the company, the main criterion individuals used to decide about union membership was whether or not they would benefit from the union contract. As the union steward who filed a union grievance explained about why he decided to join:

> If I had still been at full-time at BGS, and they hadn't cut me back to part-time, which is what they did to me, I probably wouldn't even have joined the union. I'd probably been one of those that was against it. But when I see there's nothing stopping a big company from trampling over a small employee. . . . I'm just one individual employee. All I am to them is a number, that's it. There's nothing stopping them from telling me I'm not needed anymore. If I was still full-time with the company, I wouldn't have been so gung-ho with the union. But I saw that as the only alternative to get my hours back. (20)

One hundred percent of the seventeen people who answered "yes" to the question of whether they thought the union would benefit them joined the union, while only two of the thirteen people who answered " no" became members. The same trend was found among nonunion members; nine out of the eleven claimed that the only reason they chose a nonunion status was that they felt the union was unable to provide them with the needed services. As these nonunion workers admitted:

> *Nonunion, Male Cashier:* There's nothing in it for me, maybe I'm being selfish, well, I am being selfish, but that was their whole goal anyway, to try to get more for the employee. And they couldn't have offered me anything I already didn't have. (16)
>
> *Nonunion, Female Back-Room Clerk:* So I'm still caught in the middle because I'm watching to see what happens. If it's going to be beneficial to me, then, yeah, someday down the road, I'll be a union member, just like everyone else. But to me at this point, it wasn't beneficial to join. (27)

The result of establishing the business ideology was a group of workers who held an individualist perception of the merits of the union. Workers asked themselves whether or not they would benefit from what the union had to offer and joined the union based on this criterion. Even workers who had very negative experiences during the organizing campaign admitted that their decision to join was based on a cost-benefit analysis. One union cashier, for instance, claimed that she joined the union because of the pension plan, even though organizers tried to "hit" her son:

The union reps walked in the back of the store and totally cussed my son out and swung at him to hit him. I was very much against the union. I didn't want to have anything to do with them.

Interviewer: Why did they cuss him out?
Because he told them they couldn't be back there. It was for safety's sake. The organizer told him that he could be anywhere he wanted, when he wanted, and he proceeded to cuss him out and even swung at him. Luckily my son is . . .

Interviewer: Swung at him?
Yeah, he was going to hit him. The way they acted, the things they told people, the harassment they put us through, the sarcasm—I turned against them. Now, when BGS finally accepted the union, I don't know how I felt really. Was it good for the employees, not good for the employees? I joined the union. The only reason I joined the union was that I figured it was the only logical thing to do. After being with the company for eighteen years, I wanted the security of having seniority. Plus so much of my time would turn into their pension plan that it was the only logical thing for me to do. (6)

In right-to-work states, the issue of how ideology affects members' decisions to join is important. Since workers have the option of joining the union or not, membership rates are affected by the workers' interpretation of their relationship with the union. To the degree that the unions are capable of fulfilling the needs of most employees, a ''union as business'' framework may not harm membership rates. However, a business framework detracts from the unions' attempts to create an efficacious and active workforce.

Geofelt Manufacturing

The result of excluding GM employees from the contract negotiations was a dissatisfied and, to a lesser degree, angry group who focused on their exclusion from the contract process rather than on the successes of the negotiator. Forty percent of GM employees I interviewed claimed they were dissatisfied with the contract outcome for three main reasons. First, five workers felt that the negotiator, in his haste to complete a contract, did not strategize effectively. Given that GM's slow production season was November, the three white and two African-American workers felt that they would have had more bargaining power if an agreement had not been reached until March. The workers believed that the union's disregard of the production season illustrated that it was more interested in hastening the bargaining process rather than in helping the workers. Second, two employees claimed that the new lead technician positions, which replaced assistant supervisors with rank-and-file workers, created divisions among employees. They grew suspicious of the new work arrangement when two of the four positions were filled by members of the bargaining committee. Finally, one antiunion worker, who actually benefited from the lead technician position, still argued that the contract did not change the workplace in any beneficial way. The commonality of all these complaints was a mistrust of what the union negotiator had accomplished. Since most GM workers were excluded from the process, they felt dubious that the "real" interests of the employees were met.

A second issue of exclusion, upon which 65 percent of the interviewed GM workers focused, concerned the failure to receive a copy of the union contract. When I interviewed people in February, the contract had been in effect for four months but, because of problems with the company printing the contract, the workforce had not been able to gain possession of their copies. For GM workers, not having the contract was tantamount to being powerless. As this African-American technician explained:

> Not having a contract means that we're not going to be too strong and then why have a union? Because the contract will just be used by the managers to do whatever they want and that's how they were doing it before anyway. See, if we knew what the contract said, we could have more say. One day last week I came in and took over someone's shift on my day off. I had to get home after work because my wife and I only have one car and she needed to be somewhere. I told the supervisor at 6:30 I had to go and he said I had to stay. Well, I walked away and found a union steward and he told me that the union contract says I don't have to stay. So I went home. But if I had a contract I would know myself. (7)

The feeling of weakness expressed by this worker stemmed from the absence of the instrument that he believed gave him power: the union contract. His frustration is in stark contrast to the feeling of power another African-American technician, who had a copy of the contract, attested to:

> When you go in a grievance and you know what's in the contract, you know they can't do what they're doing. It feels really good to know what can and cannot be done, and to tell them what they're doing is wrong. It feels good. They would have rewritten the contract if we would have let them. (3)

In both cases, the GM employees expressed a sense of self-efficacy, a belief that their actions were necessary. The employee with the contract stated that he felt "good" controlling the way the contract was interpreted by the company. The technician without a contract admitted that he could control his interactions with the company, yet he was structurally constrained from acting on his sense of self-efficacy because he was deprived of a contract.

Those GM workers without a contract expressed indignation about the dilemma. Invoking the "union as workers" framework, the employees argued that the union violated its exchange relationship with the workers. Workers paid union dues in exchange for more control over the workplace. Without a contract, the union was essentially useless. As the following workers explain:

> *African-American Worker:* We've been paying union dues and we still don't have a contract. The guys on the negotiating committee know some things but they can't remember the whole contract in your head. I'm paying union dues—I'd like to know what we negotiated for. (7)

> *White Worker:* That's our biggest gripe because the company goes by the contract now and every time they come up with something they say, "It's in the contract." And we just don't know if it is or not because we don't have one. We're already paying union dues. (8)

> *White Worker:* I'm getting union dues [taken] out of my check and it's not really that much to mind except the fact that I don't have any say-so. I don't get to vote on [the contract], can't get any straight answers on anything, and I don't have a contract. (11)

> *African-American Worker:* The grievances and the step procedures are all in the contract. You don't have that, you don't have anything. And then why am I paying $4.44? You can be a union member, and know just as much as the shop steward knows. (16)

Workers at GM argued that their side of the bargain was met; they were paying union dues. In exchange, however, they were not able to act on the "union as workers" framework. Indeed, they were unhappily waiting for the union to provide them with the contract. Only with the contract in hand, they believed, would they be able to control both the union and the workplace.

Several workers were unwilling to wait, however. Five vociferous workers were so angered at the way the contract unfolded that they resolved to replace the present union with one more capable of filling their needs. These five workers had been very active during the organizing campaign; one was even a member of the contract negotiations committee. However, all felt that, after the campaign succeeded, the union abandoned the workers. The most vocal member on this ad hoc committee, who also defined himself as the "most" active worker during the campaign, convinced a group of his co-workers that the clothing workers' union had proved itself unreliable and untrustworthy. He was committed to replacing the union with another. The technician had already researched the necessary steps to decertify the union, calling the National Labor Relations Board for information and approaching another union he felt would be more helpful. He explained:

> I've talked to over a dozen people and all of their opinions are the same. We have negative opinions about the union and would rather have a stronger union represent us.
> *Interviewer: What do you mean a "stronger" union?*
> Well, for one thing, I was on the bargaining committee and I still felt lost about what was happening. It was not explained to me by the union what we could or could not do. The union was just too much in a hurry and had too much on the fire to devote the time to doing what needed to be done. (5)

The technician reasoned that if the union could not provide him with the necessary education to create a strong union, he would help bring in another union that would.

The loose committee of five workers (three white and two African-American) tried to garner support by stoking anger in other union members. They spoke about the weak negotiation outcome and the failure of workers to receive contracts. While most GM workers were angry, only a minority of workers believed a new union would make a difference, so the decertification campaign eventually faded. What is notable is that the action these employees took to redress their dissatisfaction imitated the action they had engaged in to create a union. Because they had learned only the specific skills associated with conducting an organizing drive, they began another organizing campaign to replace the union.

The majority of workers at GM had faith that the union could develop strength again. Yet, at the time of my interviews, they were doing little to make change happen. As this African-American technician commented:

> I still have hope in this union. . . . See, I'm the type of person that if I know my rights, I'm gonna go after them. That's why I need a contract.

> If I know you're doing me wrong, I'm going to fight. We got some good people in the office, but with no contract to be seen, we're weak. Right now we're weak. We got a lot of people paying dues, but union-wise we're weak because no participation and not knowing what's going on. How can we do anything if we don't got any information? (7)

The technician believed that the present problem for the union was workers who were not participating as they did during the organizing campaign. His solution was to provide the rank and file with information so they would be able to act. However, he did not attempt to attain any more information than what was given to him by the union. His faith did not materialize into action. Another worker eloquently stated:

> At the time the campaign was going on . . . we finally said, "Hey, we've had enough." Then it came together, we stood up and made a change. But, since then, it's just like when you throw a rock into a pond, at first it makes a big splash, then it's just small waves ripple out. That's basically what has happened. (19)

After the "big splash," activism was slowly ebbing away. In this sense, the organizing campaign did not effectively teach the employees with "faith" that they must engage in action in order to continue the workers' strong, united front.

Dissatisfied employees were more active in trying to replace the union than "faithful" workers were in trying to rebuild the union. I think this difference in the quality and quantity of activism stems from two sources: First, most workers believed that the contract would return from the copier imminently and then they would have the capacity to build the local's strength. One worker said:

> We need to figure out how to do things now since we've never been union before. We need to get stronger and get people participating again, besides just paying union dues. We need to know what's going on, like we did during the campaign. Right now we still don't know our rights since we don't have a contract. When we get the contract and make union meetings, things are going to change. We'll see that we can do it again. (7)

The union's persistent defense that the copier would soon complete the contracts convinced most workers that waiting was a worthwhile solution to their dilemma. Since GM employees believed their strength resided in their possession of a contract, receiving a contract would certainly remedy worker nonactivism and dissatisfaction.

Second, workers had only received education about how to organize. During the campaign GM employees learned abstract principles, such as power through numbers. What they learned concretely was how to bring a union in, how to win a union election, not how to maintain solidarity after the union becomes the bargaining agent. It is not surprising that employees who were dissatisfied with the union turned to action that matched their experience of making the workplace union. This time, employees wanted to bring in a new union that would provide them with more education.

Pateman (1970) discusses in her book how employees are more comfortable with participation at the workplace when it involves their immediate job duties rather than responsibilities they have never exercised. This does not mean that workers should never participate in decision-making beyond what their job already entails, but that workers' job duties should be expanded before they are asked to participate. With labor unions, this translates into providing workers with education about unions even after the organizing campaign has been won. One white technician said:

> We really don't have . . . we got some good shop stewards, people that's trying to be good shop stewards. There's two people that are going to be very good officers, but this is the first time they've ever dealt with a union. We don't really know how to pursue the issue. *We were only trained how to get the union in.* That's why I think that the union needs to come back in and train us to handle these situations. Now, it's just, "Here's your contract. You do it." You don't know which way to go. You don't know whether . . . should I fight this issue or should I sit back and watch it? We really haven't been told how to handle the situation. (19; emphasis added)

The knowledge necessary for winning a union campaign is different from the knowledge needed to maintain a stable and strong union. For instance, before the union, workers are most concerned with keeping the workforce cohesive and separate from management so they can accomplish the shared goal of making the workplace union. After the union has been won, however, employees must juggle multiple goals and deal with management to achieve these goals. Once workers know what it means to be union, they can use this information to maintain the stability of a union.

Conclusion

Both BGS and GM workers faced similar situations during their contract negotiations. The unions controlled the creation of the contracts and failed to provide employees with the necessary education to become involved. The two work groups reacted distinctly to their exclusions, however, and I argue that the differing responses are attributable to the variable levels of participation the unions incorporated during the organizing campaigns.

The BGS campaign demonstrates that top-down institutional arrangements are capable of constraining activism across institutional settings. From its inception, the organizing campaign at BGS was controlled by union officials. The national union wanted to organize BGS so that it could help set standards for the grocery industry throughout the state of Arizona. The union focused its resources on convincing the company to accept the union rather than building worker solidarity. The lack of worker participation during the BGS campaign created two responses from the workforce. First, workers interpreted and acted towards the union as a business. When organizers interacted with BGS workers during the campaign, the contract period, and beyond, they maintained "control" over the interaction. As a result, BGS employees interpreted their role in the union strictly within the "union as business" framework. Whether or not they should participate or join the union depended on a rational, business transaction philosophy. As consumers, they should have to do very little work (activism) within the union. Indeed, workers felt that part of the union's role was discovering employees' needs; only through listening to the workers' voices could the union accurately represent their needs to the company.

Second, workers felt powerless within the union. After the campaign, BGS workers voiced dissatisfaction. Many workers were paying union dues but, in their words, not "getting what they paid for." Job instability persisted, union officials failed to return some workers' phone calls, and the majority of employees still had little knowledge of what the contract said. Yet BGS employees felt either apathetic or powerless to demand more from the union. Without knowing how the union entered the workplace or how the contract negotiations transpired, workers felt helpless to demand that the union fulfill its side of the "business" deal. In the end, then, workers desisted from activism after the campaign ended because they did not have collective experience with activism during the campaign.

The GM campaign is illustrative in that it shows how the *nature* of activism is contingent upon workers' participatory experiences in distinct institutional settings. While the union encouraged GM workers to control the organizing strategy during the campaign, the union denied participation during the contract negotiations. As a result, the majority of workers waited impatiently for the union to provide them with the education to become active, and five angry workers used the specific skills learned during the organizing campaign to attempt to reorganize the plant with another union.

I believe that general skills, such as conflict resolution and problem-solving, might help participants be active in the abstract procedures of decision-making. However, lacking the specific skills needed to reach the goal at hand—that is, creating a solid union structure—workers will not be able to control the concrete steps involved in different types of decision-making. As this African-American worker from GM said:

> We don't really know how to do anything since we've never had a union. We need guidance on how to stay more organized. We need to know how to do things to get more accomplished. (7)

Clearly, being active in a bureaucratic structure takes different resources and skills from being active in a social movement organization. For unions, this means teaching employees both how to win an election *and* how to run a union.

Empirical research on participation in the work sphere shows similar worker resistance when employees are taught participatory skills for their specific tasks but are prevented from applying these skills to broader organizational goals (Shaiken 1984; Derber and Schwartz 1983). Derber and Schwartz explain:

> [T]he relative autonomy in the labor process required to reduce worker alienation and increase worker integration also "empowers" workers psychologically to seek wider autonomy in the workplace, thereby placing strains on the existing boundaries of authority. (68)

In the present study, the "strain" on authority manifested itself in the attempt to decertify the union at GM. Clearly, then, unions eliciting participation from workers during organizing campaigns simply as a strategy to win certification elections need to consider the ramifications of participation beyond the organizing campaign.

Conclusion
Organizing as Process:
Is Participation the Solution?

Introduction

Organizing is traditionally perceived as essential for the survival of the labor movement because new members mean larger and stronger unions. Since many businesses view avoiding unions as their primary labor-management strategy, unions often use organizing outcomes as an indicator of their ability to survive. In this book, however, I have offered evidence that successful organizing campaigns do more than add members to union membership rosters. Successful campaigns are also integral for shaping workers' perceptions and actions within unions. Many union advocates intuit the relationship I have proposed without empirically examining it. For example, one study of organizing strategies suggests in its concluding remarks, "[T]he union-building approach to organizing not only allows for victory, but it also creates an opportunity to become a strong and viable union, as workers early in the organizing process gain leadership skills and understand the real power of their involvement in the union" (Bronfenbrenner and Juravich 1996, 21). My study provides both empirical support and theoretical explanation for the processual conception of organizing campaigns.

In this final chapter I explain how union organizing campaigns influence workers' perceptions and actions and describe how this process unfolded during the Comprehensive Campaign at Bob's Grocery

Stores (BGS) and the Blitz at Geofelt Manufacturing (GM). I argue that the structure of union campaigns influences, first, the establishment of union frameworks—the ways workers interpret the union's presentation-of-self, and, subsequently, workers' roles within the union (Goffman 1974). Second, campaigns provide workers with (or deprive workers of) cognitive and emotional skills for becoming active union members (Pateman 1970).

I then analyze the internal and external constraints that drive some unions to incorporate participation into their organizing strategies and other unions to exclude it. Understanding the cultural, political, and economic contexts in which unions exist helps to answer whether participation is the simple solution necessary for revitalizing the labor movement.

After the Organizing Ends

While businesses are using the rhetoric of participatory management, the truth is that many companies are cutting workers off from the company hierarchy rather than incorporating them (Moody 1988). The stripping away of human resource and participatory techniques creates a ripe opportunity for union organizing because workers are angry and frightened for their future job security. The campaigns at BGS and GM emerged within such a climate; the companies expected more work from employees while retracting familial work cultures and cutting workers' pay. As a result of the growing emotional distance between workers and managers, 85 percent of BGS workers signed union authorization cards during the last of the three employee sign-ups and 86 percent of GM employees voted for the union during their campaign election.

Before the organizing campaigns began at BGS and GM, workers did resist the distance that their companies generated. At BGS, the resistance began immediately after the new Canadian owners laid off workers. Two dozen workers met for a month to discuss organizing a union. However, these informal meetings ended when management discovered them and warned workers that a union would cost them their jobs. The cashiers I interviewed were the only workers who admitted continuing collective resistance throughout the period of deteriorating relations between workers and management. Not coincidentally, cashiers were most affected by the new company strategy;

their autonomy was severely hampered by more rules, more supervision, and less mobility. For the most part, however, the employees I interviewed said that they retaliated simply by not working as hard and not being as committed to the company. Indeed, of the twenty-five workers I interviewed who were interested in job mobility before the growing distance between workers and managers, only three still wanted to move up in the company. The rest said that, instead of moving up, they wanted to move out. This gave BGS, for the first time, a turnover rate comparable to traditional grocery stores.

At GM, the different positions and shifts kept workers from collectively mobilizing against degenerating management-labor relations before the organizing campaign. Employees resisted the increased work load and lower pay by consciously laboring less productively. One worker I interviewed admitted that, during the summer before the spring campaign began, he and two other shift workers discussed the growing problems at the company during their daily socializing near the river. However, none of these workers, nor any other workers at the company, attempted to collectively resist until the campaign began. A possible explanation for workers' hesitancy to openly rebel involves perceived upward mobility; 75 percent of the employees I interviewed aspired to ascend the job ladder. Not only did they perceive job mobility as possible once conditions improved, but employees believed company problems would dissipate as workers, themselves in particular, advanced. In fact, whereas BGS workers felt that the union's presence would help them keep the jobs they had, most GM workers envisioned the union as the necessary vehicle to help them win the opportunity to advance.

At BGS and GM, the level of cohesion was similar among workers before the campaigns; both workforces saw their relationship to the company in individual rather than collective terms. During the union organizing campaign at BGS, the workers' sense of individualism deepened as they began to relate to the union within a strictly business framework. The rules of the Comprehensive Campaign, as practiced by the grocery workers' union, required BGS employees to play a minimal role during the campaign. Organizers restricted the activism of employees by allowing less than 1 percent of the workforce to fully participate. The union did not establish any store-wide or company-wide collective activities during the entire twenty-month campaign. Instead of collective mobilization, organizers asked workers simply to sign, and encourage other workers to sign, authorization cards. These cards were secondary to the union's primary task of collecting negotiable information about the company.

The BGS organizers purposefully invoked a "union as business" framework. As instructed by union officials, organizers were to attain many workers' signatures quickly. The workers I interviewed claimed that, in their pursuit to complete the job, organizers acted like pushy salesmen concerned only with completing the transaction rather than with developing a relationship with workers. One scanning coordinator who joined the union commented:

> When the union organizers came into the store, they would fish around to try to find out what people were bitching and complaining about, and then they would say, "We'll fix that if you sign this card." They just went to the stores to get cards signed, they didn't care what they had to say to get those cards signed. (1)

As this worker noted, organizers appealed to employees' sense of practicality; the union would "fix" their economic insecurity if they signed the card. With that type of interaction repeated throughout the campaign, the union secured its own image as a business.

At GM, workers' individualist conception of the workplace was transformed during the organizing campaign as employees collectively mobilized and established a "union as workers" framework. The Blitz requires that the entire campaign conclude quickly so that the company does not have time to successfully build an offensive against the union. To hasten the process, the organizer at GM immediately called at workers' homes, using a list he attained through an employee. However, because he was excluded from the workplace, the organizer depended upon GM workers to generate activism and union education throughout the campaign. Workers perceived the organizer as imperative for two reasons: (1) he provided workers a place to congregate, which allowed employees to collectively voice ideas and concerns, and (2) he educated workers about the steps the company would take to thwart the campaign—which allowed workers to develop a shared counteractive strategy. All workers, even those against the union, believed the election outcome depended on the joint effort of GM employees.

The production of a collectivist mentality did not transform GM workers into radicals ready to challenge the capitalist system. Rather, workers perceived their unified activities as a necessary tool for providing them with the same instrumental rewards that BGS workers desired: job security and more money. One union worker said:

> We just went out and told people what the deal was. If they wanted better conditions for everyone and better raises, then we'd have to get together and do something about it. 'Cause you can't do it alone. There's strength in numbers. We talked about that quite a bit. If it was just going to be five or six people involved in the whole thing, there wasn't really much to pursue. The organizers told us the only way we could do it was by getting the help of all the workers 'cause that's what the union is, the workers, and if we don't stand together now, we'll never stand together. (10)

The goal was the same for both BGS and GM workers. However, the processes differed. The organizer taught GM workers that to attain economic rewards they had to act together. Through their collective endeavors, GM workers created the image of the "union as the workers."

The unions' presentation-of-self offered workers not only frameworks by which employees were taught to perceive the unions, but also sets of real skills through which workers learned their roles within the unions. Pateman's claim is that institutional arrangements provide participants with emotional and cognitive skills and that these skills direct the shape and scope of action. Hierarchical institutional arrangements teach workers that activism is inappropriate; thus, action is constrained and, when manifested, short-lived (1970).

At BGS, workers interpreted the union-controlled organizing campaign within the business framework. Organizers presented themselves as professionals whom employees could rely on to complete the job. Individual workers had the small role of completing assignments when asked by the union. However, workers believed their role as consumers allowed them the luxury of letting the professionals complete the job. Most BGS employees did not see collective activism as their role within the campaign. Instead, organizers performed the primary task of creating a union at BGS. As a result, workers lacked the most fundamental participatory skills during the campaign. Indeed, they could not even explain how the union won the campaign at BGS except through visions of a corrupt and undemocratic union.

After the campaign ended, the business framework continued to color workers' perceptions of the union during the contract period and beyond. The business paradigm became so ubiquitous that workers used it to understand and justify their lack of participation within the union. I describe three primary ways in which BGS workers invoked the business framework to legitimize their nonparticipation. The first concerns the issue of "voice." The majority of BGS employees whom I interviewed declared that they should have a right to voice within the union. However, theirs was a passive conception of voice: in order for organizers to meet the workers' needs and provide them with the goods they wanted, organizers needed to survey each of them. The BGS employees' idea of voice, then, forced organizers to be active in serving the needs and desires of the passive workforce.

However, even within this passive conception of voice, workers were sometimes required to be active, if only momentarily, in order to defend breaches associated with the business framework. For instance, one BGS worker recalled that he and twenty other workers collectively demanded from the union that they be able to choose a shop steward, someone they trusted to represent their needs to the union. Yet when the union ignored their request, employees refrained from further activism. Employees may not have liked the union breaching their implicit contract about voice but, without participatory skills, workers believed it more realistic to narrow their idea of "voice" rather than expand it.

The second way BGS workers used the business framework to legitimize their nonparticipation concerned decisions about joining the union. Organizers "sold" the union with claims that workers' individual economic positions would improve after the campaign. Employees thus decided to join the union using one main criterion: whether or not they would benefit financially. Workers put aside their rancor towards the union and instead relied on a simple cost-benefit analysis to help them make their decision. For instance, one carry-out explained that her positive opinion of unions was dramatically altered during the campaign. She claimed that she developed an antiunion sentiment after organizers acted pushy and seemed solely interested in procuring signatures on cards. Yet, when I asked her what the union could do to convince her to become a member, she answered:

> Get something that benefited me. A raise, but more than just ten cents. (11)

Employees of BGS justified decisions not to join, or to join, the union within a context of business unionism. Workers who saw no immediate individual benefit from becoming a member felt legitimate in withholding their dues from the union.

Finally, BGS workers articulated a strong apprehension about becoming active in the union because their previous experiences taught them that activism was both inappropriate and futile. One BGS employee, who had been active during the first, defunct, worker-run organizing campaign, said:

> I don't need to become involved. We pay people to do that. We pay our leaders to find out what our needs are. We pay organizers and the president to make sure our needs are taken care of. If they're doing their jobs, I shouldn't have to participate. (1)

With the campaign complete, workers still perceived their role in the union as that of the consumer in an economic transaction, a consumer with little recourse but to "grin and bear" the decisions of the powerful "business." Even when BGS employees wanted to exit the union, they felt inefficacious to do so. Since they had no knowledge of how the union entered the business, they did not develop the skills to force the union out. For many employees, the union became another powerful organization that created rules over which they had no control.

Institutional arrangements that incorporate participation in decision-making create workers different from the kind of passive "victims" described above. When organizational participants are required to become active, they develop both the general and specific skills to diffuse participation and the emotional efficacy to disseminate those skills (Pateman 1970).

During the GM campaign, workers shared the task of winning the election with the organizer. The organizer clearly had more experience with campaigns, so employees respected his advice. However, because they shared decision-making with the organizer, workers developed a "union as workers" framework. Employees of GM were so convinced that their actions were crucial in generating the outcome that both pro- and antiunion workers developed committees in charge of educating workers and organizing collective action. Furthermore, since prounion workers believed that the strongest unions came from a unified workforce, they felt justified in "pressuring" ambivalent workers to go to meetings and social activities. As a result of the high level of participation, all workers experienced a new set of emotional and cognitive organizing skills. In addition to undergoing an enhancement in group efficacy, most employees learned the specific steps it took to win an election and the general importance of creating worker cohesion.

After the campaign ended, however, the participatory democratic structure slowly fell apart. Due to limited resources and time constraints, the contract negotiations were controlled mainly by union officials and the company. While a democratically elected workers' negotiation committee appeared for contract talks, they did not understand the discourse exchanged by the two parties and thus felt unable to participate in it. Cohesion among employees deteriorated when the rank and file accused the negotiating committee of withholding information from them. The contract negotiation period, then, was not a time for expanding workers' education about unionism. However, even though the participatory democratic structure degenerated after the campaign ended, both the "union as workers" framework and the skills workers learned during the campaign survived. I talk about three ways workers legitimized the diffusion of skills using the "union as workers" framework.

First, GM workers expressed a continued sense of efficacy. Directly after the campaign's completion, employees believed that their control within the workplace grew. Workers reported feeling more confident in approaching supervisors with suggestions and complaints. Even three to five months after the contract talks, when employees still did not have access to the union contract, workers voiced a strong belief in their power to create change. The problem was that, without the rules of interaction expressed within the contract, employees felt structurally constrained from acting on their feelings of efficacy. Most GM workers concurred that their sense of control was enhanced as a function of the campaign. However, the union's failure to provide them with copies of the contract impeded the transformation of their efficacy into action. Furthermore, they interpreted the union's failure as a breach in the "union as workers" framework that the union itself had helped to establish. Employees were paying union dues and, in exchange, felt they deserved control over the workplace.

A second way the diffusion of skills manifested was through increased activism within the workplace. Individually, not only did workers feel efficacious, but 20 percent of the employees I interviewed claimed that since the campaign they had voiced concerns about their own positions to the supervisors at the plant and 10 percent reported finally defending their co-workers. Collectively, twelve African-American men at the plant sued the company for race discrimination. Although many of these workers felt discrimination had existed since the inception of the company, the skills generated during the campaign finally motivated them to take action. The technician who helped file the class-action suit said:

> I told my supervisor, "There's a lot of injustice going on here, and something's gonna be done about it, especially now that the campaign was won and we did it." Two days later, I called the lawyers. (16)

Workers understood the power that evolved from unified action.

Finally, five GM workers took the specific skill, how to organize a campaign, and attempted, unsuccessfully, to decertify the union. The workers' decertification movement emerged from a breakdown in the participatory democratic rules established by the union. Fantasia argues that activism is often an organic expression that evolves when formal organizational rules break down (1988). The "union as workers" framework established rights of worker control. When the union violated these rights by preventing participation during the contract period and failing to educate workers about unionism, a few GM employees rebelled. The action they inspired among themselves mimicked the actions they took to organize the workplace because these were the only skills they had practiced.

Employees did not know how to generate "positive" activism within the union structure because they had no experience within that structure. Indeed, workers with faith in the union admitted that only if communication increased among members could the union regain strength. Many hopeful workers believed the turning point would come with the imminent arrival of the union contracts.

The union-controlled organizing campaign at BGS established a business framework among employees. Workers viewed worker cohesion and activism as superfluous to their role within the campaign. Instead, they held the union responsible for fulfilling their needs. When the union failed to do so, workers remained passive because they did not have the skills to produce action. The worker-controlled campaign at GM invoked an entirely different set of rules about who should control the union and fostered the emergence of the "union as workers'' framework. Employees believed they had a right to a contract. However, because they had only learned the participatory skill of establishing an election, five workers resorted to a decertification campaign to recoup what they perceived as their legitimate right to power. Participation, then, is a tool that can empower workers, but it can also harm unions when the institutional arrangements supporting it degenerate. Companies introducing participatory workplaces have also seen a backlash from participants when the collective decision-making structure fades or exists only rhetorically (Shaiken 1984; Derber and Schwartz 1983).

The theory of participatory democracy explains how institutional arrangements influence workers' cognitive and behavioral responses. However, it neglects to consider how organizational participants construct meaning from their structural situations. A more comprehensive understanding of structure entails incorporating how participants produce personal meaning from organizations. This book demonstrates that union campaigns mediate workers' perceptions of the unions and, subsequently, their levels of activism after the campaigns end.

Unions historically have been committed to worker activism for ideological reasons. Indeed, unions differentiate themselves from businesses based on their commitment to worker control. A 1985 report published by the AFL-CIO chastises the labor movement for not making its worker-centered ideology more manifest; the labor movement must cogently convey that ''unions are democratic institutions controlled by their members'' (13). Clearly, the motive to present themselves as the true ''voice'' of laborers involves more than ideology. Unions also hope to build trust in the labor movement and entice more workers to join. Furthermore, Bronfenbrenner's extensive work on organizing campaigns shows that worker participation yields other practical results besides attracting new members; activism also increases the odds of winning union elections (1997).

If worker participation is crucial to the image and the survival of the labor movement, it is unclear why unions do not incorporate activism more intricately into their organizing strategies. While this book does not empirically address the question why unions choose certain organizing strategies in order to avoid facile solutions for unions, it is imperative to understand the context in which unions make decisions.

Is Participation the Panacea?

Unions have been accused of creating their own troubles by failing to incorporate active worker participation into the labor movement. For instance, two labor advocates, Jeremy Brecher and Tim Costello, claim:

> Those who now lead the AFL-CIO likewise must encourage dramatic change or see their own organizations plunge toward extinction. They might prefer to have change limited to a militant business unionism which combines top-down control with more vigorous organizing and a greater willingness to strike. Nevertheless, any substantial revitalization of the labor movement will require a move toward social movement unionism, in which grassroots activism supplants the rigid, bureaucratic character all too typical of American trade unions. (1996, 8)

If participation is truly the panacea, then unions that fail to foster worker participation seem irrational and morally responsible for their own waning strength. However, if we take into account the sociopolitical environment in which unions are operating, we may understand the reasons why many unions fail to incorporate participatory democracy.

In order to generate a rank-and-file union campaign, organizing strategies must incorporate a structure that develops both worker leadership and union consciousness (Bronfenbrenner and Juravich 1996, 5). In the United States, active business opposition supported by weak government policies makes it difficult for unions to generate these fundamental aspects of worker-controlled campaigns. First, companies are likely to benefit from illegally avoiding unions. Two illegal actions, for example, that harm worker leadership and union consciousness are firing prounion workers and bad-faith bargaining. The consequences for companies that fire prounion workers are a monetary fine by the NLRB and an order to reinstate the worker. However, as one recent study shows, only 34 percent of workers fired for union activity are reinstated before the union election (Bronfenbrenner 1994), and the financial costs of fines are much smaller for the company than the perceived economic costs of recognizing a union. Unions have a difficult time attracting and maintaining a solid leadership base when workers are threatened or actually fired.

Once the union attains bargaining rights for workers, it must still develop a contract. A resisting company can avoid a contract by refusing to negotiate. The harshest penalty a business receives from the NLRB is an order to end their bad-faith bargaining (Kochan, Katz, and McKersie 1986). A stalemate between the company and union affects employee morale. Research confirms that contract delays injure worker solidarity and increase the likelihood that employees decertify a union (Freeman 1985). Given the weak penalties that businesses accrue from engaging in illegal union-avoidance strategies, it is not surprising that unfair labor practices have grown over the last thirty years (Freeman 1985).

The NLRB also affords companies legal strategies of union deterrence that harm worker leadership and union consciousness. Businesses have the right to hold captive audience meetings to "inform" workers how unions could potentially harm the company. Furthermore, management can pull individual workers off the floor to "talk" one-on-one about company attitudes towards the union. These strategies not only create fear in workers, although the company may not have issued any direct threats, but also serve to divide and conquer employees, all of whom are worried about their economic future. Since unions have no legal access to workers in the plant, they face a great challenge in generating union consciousness within an anti-union environment.

Unions can overcome these obstacles to win union elections. Indeed, worker participation is one such strategy that can help defeat business resistance (Bronfenbrenner 1997). However, some unions may rationally choose top-down strategies precisely to avoid the "negative" effects of business opposition. For example, one organizer I interviewed from the grocery workers' campaign justified using the Comprehensive Campaign because:

> Companies will do anything to keep a union out. They'll fire prounion people. One of the reasons we don't like elections is because there are several law firms around the country that are particularly scummy. Companies hire lawyers that will help them do dirty rotten things to employees. . . . We like to avoid that. (2)

Furthermore, this organizer argued that the Comprehensive Campaign is an effective strategy for winning recognition in the workplace. He argued, "Given the way the Board (NLRB) is right now, it is incredibly difficult to win an election so the best way is through voluntary recognition." Another organizer who worked on the Comprehensive Campaign at BGS corroborated:

> We prefer to go the voluntary recognition route because the way the labor
> case law has been for the past years is totally for the employer. They can
> appeal, use their right to appeal and litigate and stall and drag their feet
> and it can be before you even had an election, depending [on] how much
> money the company wanted to spend. (5)

Rationally, then, the grocery workers' union chooses the Comprehensive Campaign because it perceives the top-down strategy as most effective at winning union contracts in the present antiunion climate.

Organizers from the clothing workers' campaign justified their choice of strategy for precisely the same reason. One of the organizers claimed:

> The campaign you just came from, Geofelt was . . . they were involved in
> a very basic way. We never passed out a leaflet. They ran their meetings,
> they participated all the way through the campaign. The "why" part is
> that it is their organization, right? So it's logical that from the beginning
> you want to create as much of that as you could. But also besides being
> the right thing and the principled thing to do, it's what makes it possible
> to win, you create that ownership. . . . I think that one huge factor in the
> ability to win is the ability to have real leaders who are involved in the
> campaign, have ownership in the campaign, and are involved in every step
> of the way. Things may have changed in that it may not have been as
> necessary when the environment was more level. It's a necessity now. (3)

All of the organizers I interviewed perceived that an antiunion political climate had developed since the beginning of the Reagan administration. Their answer to increased resistance to unions was to establish organizing strategies that they believed worked. For them, the choice of top-down versus bottom-up campaigns was a matter of survival. As one organizer from the grocery workers' campaign admitted, "We're useless to them unless we win that contract."

A second factor that helps explain unions' choices in organizing strategies stems from the union organization itself. A recent study by Voss and Sherman shows that unions are more likely to incorporate new, innovative strategies, including worker activism, when the top union hierarchy advocates a shift in resources to organizing. The study noted that the UFCW was a "partial innovator," but it failed to include worker participation within its organizing strategies. Voss and Sherman explain that "partial innovators" lack the monetary resources to contribute to organizing. Furthermore, the culture within such unions deflects a shift from union-controlled to worker-controlled campaigns (1997, 23). Unions that historically desist from worker participation within the union structure are more likely to maintain that culture within their organizing campaigns. Like companies, then, unions are prone to organizational inertia.

A combination of both external and internal constraints influences a union's choice of organizing strategy. Externally, unions are operating in an economic and political climate that favors businesses. Internally, unions possess their own historical cultures that shape the solutions they create to overcome resistance towards unions. Theoretically, the Comprehensive Campaign could be made more participatory just as the Blitz could be made more union-controlled. Realistically, however, unions are embedded within social contexts that constrain their behavior. Thus, even while worker participation seems like a plausible solution to the declining labor movement, its treatment as a panacea ignores the social forces that shape unions' choices.

Conclusion

Unions organize to win. The strategies they apply to win their campaigns emerge from both external and internal sources. In this study, I have tried to show that winning a campaign is not all a union does when it organizes a workplace. Through the process of organizing, workers develop frameworks that set the stage for future interactions between the union and the workforce. Furthermore, the institutional arrangements established during the course of the campaign influence the types of skills workers develop. Together, the frameworks and the skills shape the quantity and quality of worker activism after the campaigns' end. As an organizer for the clothing workers perceived:

> It all has to do with the way the campaign was structured in the beginning, and the follow-up with the rep that works with them. If the campaign at the beginning is about a struggle, a real workers' struggle, and workers struggle together, and they learn how to communicate, they learn how to come together, they learn how to form their own organization—that's a mighty good way to start off a union. It teaches them how to be on their own and that's what you need to have a successful union. (3)

If worker empowerment is the goal of the labor movement, evidence from this study supports that beginning workers' union experiences with activism is the solution. The question that unions must address is how to incorporate worker participation in both a business and union culture that only ambivalently supports it.

Appendix
A Note on Methodology

During the Bob's Grocery Stores (BGS) campaign, I met three teachers from the Organizing Institute who were at the campaign to instruct new organizers. Having trained students for several of the affiliated AFL-CIO unions, these people had experience with a variety of organizing strategies. One strategy that the three leaders kept referring to as grass-roots-oriented was called the Blitz, used by the clothing workers' union. Sally, one of the leaders, told me that a wonderful comparative study would entail the Comprehensive Campaign and the Blitz. She encouraged me to attend a Blitz organizing campaign in Louisiana that was to take place in the middle of November. Sally said she knew the organizers for the campaign and could guarantee me entry if I attended. I agreed to attend.

Meanwhile, I spent a total of ten days at the BGS organizing campaign attending strategy meetings, joining organizers for meals and recreation, and riding with them to the stores as they spoke with BGS employees. I informally interviewed organizers as I spent time with them. I was mainly interested in finding out if the Comprehensive Campaign was really a top-down strategy and how the organizers felt about it. I also helped out with the campaign by doing card checks, making sure that the people who signed cards were actually employees at BGS. This entailed calling the employees on the phone to confirm that they did indeed sign cards. Finally, I formally interviewed five organizers from BGS. I was interested in knowing the history of the Comprehensive Campaign. How did it develop? Who first thought of it? Were other unions using this technique? Through these formal interviews, I obtained the entire history of the BGS campaign.

In November 1992, I flew to Lafayette, Louisiana. For ten days I witnessed the latter stages of the Blitz campaign at a company with five thousand clothing employees. The initial stages of the Blitz had already taken place ten days before. At that time about one hundred volunteer and paid organizers went to employees' homes trying to collect signatures. Unfortunately, the Blitz had failed, meaning that organizers did not collect the necessary 30 percent of the workers' signatures to file for an NLRB election. Organizers attributed the failure of the Blitz to their inability to obtain any type of list of the workers' names. Without a list, organizers were forced into going door-to-door, asking residents if they worked at the plant and, if not, if they knew anyone who did. This ad hoc strategy made it difficult to speak to many workers in a three-day period. Although the Blitz had failed, organizers decided to plow ahead with the campaign, hoping to familiarize the workforce with the union so a future Blitz campaign would be more successful. By the time I arrived, organizers were aware that their gains were slight, yet they organized the continuing campaign as if the Blitz had been a success. The ''after-Blitz'' campaign had been in action seven days before I came onto the scene.

I drove to the motel from the airport just in time to take part in a union organizing strategy meeting. I saw several familiar people at the meeting, one of whom was Sally, the teacher from the Organizing Institute who had told me about the campaign. The other two, Steve and Ted, were students who had also participated at BGS and were now completing their second internship with the Organizing Institute.

This meeting was obviously different from any meeting I witnessed during the BGS campaign. First, organizers sat around a huge table rather than sitting classroom fashion with the lead organizers up front. Second, discussion centered on the workforce, not on the number of cards being signed. The organizers were attempting to establish a workers' committee, a dedicated group of workers who would also act as organizers. Therefore, their conversation emphasized the interactions they had with employees. Did the employee show an interest in participating or volunteer to do any work? Third, organizers discussed ideas that employees had shared with them about how to get more workers involved in the campaign.

A few days later, I noticed that the differences between the two campaigns involved much more than meeting styles. The largest difference was the interactions between workers and organizers. The clothing workers' organizers spent time with the employees at their homes answering questions about the union, as well as engaging in social activities and conversation. We sometimes ate with workers, and some organizers even went to church with them.

I wondered immediately if the differences in campaign styles that I perceived were obvious to Steve and Ted. On my fifth day, I separately interviewed both students (who had been in Louisiana seven days longer than I had). I asked if they had noticed any similarities or differences between the Blitz and the Comprehensive Campaign. Steve answered:

> They're totally different campaigns. The clothing workers' union is serious about organizing. Grocery workers' are top-down, they have no concern with the workers. They didn't encourage us to build workers' committees or anything. The clothing workers' union encourages us to get to know the workers and build organizations to help people get involved.

Ted responded similarly:

> It didn't seem like the grocery workers' union was interested in the people. They just wanted the money. Here, they're really trying to build something.

Both Steve and Ted corroborated my perception that the two campaigns were indeed different.

I spent the last days of my stay formally interviewing three of the paid clothing organizers and two instructors from the Organizing Institute. My interest, once again, was in discovering more about the Blitz campaign. Who created it? What did organizers think about it? Were other unions using it? I also continued to ride around with the organizers as they spoke with workers and informally interviewed them during our time together.

Upon my return from Louisiana, I reviewed all the information I had collected about the two campaigns. Before making a final decision to use these campaigns as representatives of top-down and bottom-up strategies, I talked with two labor academics and two organizers from other union organizations. The academics, Kate Bronfenbrenner and Virginia duRivage, were active both in the labor movement and academia. The organizers were members of the Service Employees International Union and the Teamsters. On the phone, I asked all four to give me examples of organizing strategies that fell into the authoritative versus the grass-roots categories. They all answered that the clothing workers' union, among several others, such as Justice for Janitors, Teamsters, and SEIU, were known for involving employees. The grocery workers' union had a more top-down reputation. Given the interviews I had collected, my own experiences, and the information gained from these phone calls, I finally decided to choose the Comprehensive Campaign and the Blitz strategies to analyze how top-down versus bottom-up strategies influenced workers' sentiments and actions.

I faced two constraints in deciding which workplaces would be best for interviewing workers. First, since I was interested in the activism of employees in the union after the organizing campaign, I had to choose workplaces in which organizing campaigns were successful and contracts were successfully negotiated. Choosing successful campaigns and contract negotiations assured me that any negative attitudes expressed by employees would not be caused by the outcome of the campaign or the inability to secure a contract. This constraint meant that I could not interview the clothing employees from the campaign in Louisiana, since the union had not won the election. However, I could interview workers from the BGS campaign, which resulted in a unionized company and a contract in December 1992. The second constraint of choice in workplace arose because the BGS campaign took place in a right-to-work state. Therefore, I needed to choose a second workplace that was also located in a state with lower than average unionism.

Taken together, these two constraints made finding a second case a daunting task. While the clothing workers' had won many elections in right-to-work states, none had been able to secure a contract as of the beginning of 1993, which is when I wanted to begin my discussions with workers. I decided to proceed with my interviews of BGS workers and, hopefully, find a second case in the process.

Participation in classes at the University prevented me from beginning my interviews of BGS employees until May 1993. I was fortunate enough to obtain a list of all employees, which included their hire dates, addresses, phone numbers, and union status. This allowed me to randomly choose subjects to interview. I limited the population to employees who were eligible to sign union authorization cards and had been present for the entire campaign period, plus contract negotiations. This reduced the population from forty-two hundred to twenty-two hundred (or about ninety workers from each of the twenty-four stores). Twenty-two hundred was still a hefty number, so the representatives from the union suggested I choose one store from each of the various geographical regions in the city to pick the sample, utilizing purposive cluster sampling (Babbie 1995). The organizers believed geography was an appropriate way to divide the city because each section represented different cultural viewpoints. For instance, stores on the southwest side were located in the Latino area, where workers tended to be radical; stores centrally located employed mainly college students, who also tended to be rebellious; stores in the northeast, the wealthier part of town, were conservative; stores in the southeast were also conservative because of the residents' religious convictions; and, finally, stores in the northwest served mainly the rural areas of Phoenix. After dividing the stores into the different areas, I then randomly chose one store to represent each of the five specific geographical regions. Once the stores were chosen, I called every tenth person on the list to set up an interview.

Theoretically, the method I used to select subjects was very sound. Practically, however, I had problems. First, I called the company before I began interviewing to obtain permission to talk to employees at the stores about my project. In person, I felt I could convince workers that I was a researcher interested in their opinions; I could give them my card and a letter from my dissertation committee chair to attain some legitimacy as a social scientist. However, the company denied me access to the stores. Second, with access denied, I had to approach subjects solely through phone calls. As mentioned earlier, I had obtained a phone list of all the workers from an informant. However, my informant wished to remain discreet. This created a disadvantage for me in that subjects were very suspicious as to how I obtained their phone numbers. Sixty percent of the employees had unlisted numbers and believed the only way I could have obtained their numbers was through the company. Many did not believe that I was an independent researcher interested in their experiences in "the changing workplace." As a result, I had to expand my sample list from one to three stores in each of the five geographical areas. With this technique, I successfully interviewed fifteen subjects by calling every tenth worker in the fifteen stores. I noticed quickly that although people came from different stores, their responses to the campaign were markedly similar. With this in mind, I decided to cap the number of interviews at thirty.

At the midway point, I also discovered that I was having a difficult time gathering data from nonunion, nonwhite workers. I had anticipated this problem and, in earlier interviews, asked subjects for names of their co-workers with nonunion and nonwhite status. I interviewed ten people, then, through snowball sampling.

I completed the thirty interviews of BGS grocery workers in August 1993. Each interview followed the same format and included the same questions. I met workers at their homes or at restaurants, whichever was most convenient for them. The interview sessions were recorded on tape and lasted, on average, two hours. During the summer and fall, I transcribed the interviews onto a computer, which allowed me a hard copy of all the discussions. I then coded the interviews into sixty-two overlapping categories of interest.

By the end of the fall semester, I was ready to collect interviews from workers who had experienced an as yet unidentified Blitz campaign. In January 1994, I decided that I could no longer wait for some of the campaigns I had thought would be a good match in terms of gender and race. (For example, there was a campaign in Nashville, Tennessee, which matched perfectly with the BGS campaign in terms of size, race and gender. However, the election had been won over a year ago, and there was still no sign that the company would agree to a contract.) I decided to interview workers from a geotextile company in a rural Alabama town that had agreed on a contract with the union in November 1993. While Geofelt Manufacturing (GM) employed only one hundred workers, this was comparable to the size of one grocery store. Plus, I did not perceive that the clothing workers' union had an advantage at creating a more participatory campaign as far as labor and worker characteristics were concerned (see Chapter 3).

In order to learn about the GM campaign, I talked with the union representative in the area and the organizer who had helped conduct the campaign. These people were helpful in providing a history of the company and the way the campaign was structured. I left for the company site in late February 1994. I drove to the research site; having a car provided me the opportunity to go to the workers rather than making them come to me for an interview. Once in the area, I procured a list of all the employees at the company from an informant who wished to remain anonymous. The list contained each worker's phone number, shift, and union status. I wished to speak only with employees who had been part of the bargaining unit and who had been at the plant during the entire organizing campaign and the contract period. This narrowed the population to seventy workers.

I had a much lower rejection rate when I called GM workers for an interview (zero people said ''no''), a benefit of doing research in a rural community where people are not yet jaded by strangers calling them. In fact, four of the employees who were not home when I phoned called me back long-distance, even though they had no idea who I was or why I called them. I randomly selected the names for interviews by calling every third person on the list. In five cases, I was unable to reach a person after several phone calls so I moved down the list without waiting for a response. I also had a difficult time reaching workers who were not in the union. Previous subjects I spoke with had given me names of all the nonunion people they knew, so I interviewed the nonunion people through snowball sampling rather than through random sampling.

While my goal was to interview thirty people in this group, I noticed that I was not getting any new material after speaking with the first fifteen union members, so I decided to end the interviews after my twentieth subject. In total, I was in Alabama for one month speaking with employees from GM. Once home, I transcribed the interviews onto a computer and coded the data, as I did with the BGS discussions.

Notes

Introduction. After the Organizing Ends

1. This logic is indeed true when the signed authorization cards are used to set up an NLRB election. The employee can sign a card and still decide to vote ''no'' in the election. However, during the Comprehensive Campaign, the signed card is, in essence, a vote for the union. Thus, by not informing the workers that their cards will be used in an attempt to convince the company to recognize the union without going to an election, signing a card can ''hurt'' the employees if they are against or ambivalent towards the union.

2. The most comprehensive study is Bronfenbrenner's (1993) quantitative survey measuring union campaign characteristics and management strategies during organizing drives. Her most notable finding is that when unions involve workers in the campaign, elections are more likely to favor the unions, even when management attempts to thwart the union with a drive of its own. Case studies, which richly describe the process of involving workers in the campaign drive, further corroborate the relationship between worker participation and campaign successes (Hurd and Rouse 1989; Hurd and McElwain 1988; Hurd 1986).

3. Both company names, Bob's Grocery Stores (BGS) and Geofelt Manufacturing (GM), are pseudonyms.

Chapter 1. Historical Challenges and Contemporary Innovations

1. Ironically, some scholars interpret the passage of the National Labor Relations Act (NLRA) as a government strategy meant to eviscerate growing labor unrest rather than a first attempt at pro-labor legislation (Domhoff 1990; Goldfield 1989; Rubin 1986; Hurd 1976). In the early thirties, the United States witnessed a large swell of strike activity among workers, led by communists. Businesses were unable to contain worker resistance, regardless of their traditional strategies. Domhoff and Goldfield provide evidence that some powerful businesses actively supported the passage of the Wagner Act, reasoning that, with the legitimation of union organizing,

there would be no need for labor militancy and, thus, radical elements creating up-heaval would lose their power. Thus, even the Wagner Act, the first piece of seem-ingly pro-labor legislation, embodied successful business resistance towards radical union activists.

2. Right-to-work laws force the union to provide all workers benefits and repre-sentation, but do not require that employees join the union in order to receive those services.

3. Furthermore, businesses have been so successful at defining unions as harmful that even companies without financial problems have used "high wages" as a justi-fication for laying off workers. For example, the high profit levels at IBM and AT&T did not prevent these companies from layoffs in the eighties and nineties.

4. Information about traditional campaigns comes from Stanley Rostov's 1948 Master's thesis, "Factors Affecting the Success of Union Organizing Efforts," and Barbash's *Labor Unions in Action* (1948).

5. What makes these strategies new is not necessarily their innovation. Histori-cally, unions could and did attempt variations of the traditional campaign. However, the unions I discuss are using the new strategies in a systematic way with most of their campaigns, rather than haphazardly with a few campaigns.

Chapter 2. Participatory Democracy:
Its Possibilities and Consequences

1. A counterexample of this is Stepan-Norris and Zeitlin's (1991) article focusing on what happens to union contracts when unions are democratic, rather than whether or not democracy in unions is possible.

2. For excellent empirical studies about the mechanisms necessary to overcome oligarchy, see Lipset, Trow, and Coleman's (1956) classic study, *Union Democracy,* as well as Cornfield's (1986) explanation of the rise of women and minorities in the furniture workers' union and Stepan-Norris and Zeitlin's (1996) account of the com-munist influence in the CIO.

3. For example, Lester (1958) notes the decreased radicalism of the CIO in the 1950s without explaining that the radicalism had existed primarily because of the communists and that the communists were expelled from the union by CIO officials in the mid-forties (Stepan-Norris and Zeitlin 1991).

4. The idea that humans desire control over their lives stems from guild socialists' assumption of human nature (Cole 1928, 1920). I earlier stated that advocates of participatory democracy refute classical liberal assumptions that human nature is static. Viewing humans as dynamic does not conflict with the notion that individuals desire control over their lives. This is because ultimately Pateman and her contem-poraries see humans as easily adaptable, but preferring control over their own fate.

5. The proposition that activism is more enjoyable to people than passiveness stems from the assumption discussed in the previous endnote. Since the idea is simple and easy to test, I do not spend time discussing it.

6. Pateman breaks the cognitive skill into "higher" and "lower" levels of par-ticipation rather than general and specific. Her distinction corresponds to where, in the organizational hierarchy, people are given information and decision-making power. Mason refers to "scope" and "intensity." These terms differ minimally from my own. I use general and specific because they imply levels of experience with

decision-making power. For example, a worker who has only specific knowledge probably has not had opportunities for decision-making.

Chapter 3. Conflict and Cohesion: Worker Activism Before the Organizing Campaigns

1. However, fifty percent of workers did say they spoke out when they felt they were treated unfairly. I talk about these workers below, within the section ''workers' ideologies and attitudes.''

2. Many studies define militancy through the willingness of workers to join unions. However, as my case studies demonstrate, successfully bargaining for a union contract does not necessarily mean that workers are active in bringing the union in. Thus, I see activism in the organizing campaign or resistance at work as different from simply being part of a workgroup that joined a union.

3. Forty percent of BGS workers interviewed were married and 53 percent had children.

4. Of the thirty people I interviewed, three people had family members who also worked at BGS. Two cashiers had sons who were stockers and one cashier's father worked in the meat department.

5. Men and women in gender atypical jobs were very rare. Of the thirty people I interviewed, two men were cashiers and one women worked in the back of the store in receiving.

6. Pineville is a pseudonym.

7. The town consisted of two grocery stores, laundromats/video stores, hardware/gift stores, diners, and clothing stores. Yet one-fifth of the storefronts were boarded up and empty.

8. For instance, one day as I strolled through one of the neighborhoods, a policeman stopped me, asked me for my car registration, queried why I was walking, and then told me, ''We don't walk around here so I don't want to see you out here again.'' Afterwards I stationed myself in the town cemetery, where I was left alone.

9. One of these men became a member of the organizing committee during the campaign.

10. Older workers also tended to have worked at the plant longer, which probably explained why they were more likely to know people from different shifts.

11. However, three tenured workers (two black) said they resented how younger workers were moving up more quickly than they were.

12. In this section, I bring up gender and race only when men/women at BGS and whites/African-Americans at GM register different responses to the same questions.

13. The average length of employment for the employees that I interviewed was eight years. Yet here I must note that I only interviewed people who experienced the entire twenty-month campaign, plus five months of its aftermath; thus, all the people I interviewed had been with BGS at least twenty-five months.

14. Of the three people who wished to move up, one was a woman.

15. More women (two-thirds) than men (one-half) defined themselves as rebellious.

16. Since I spoke with employees who had experienced the campaign, the contract

period and three to five months since the contract period, all workers I interviewed had been with the company for twenty-five months or more.

17. Slightly more African-Americans (seven out of nine) said they desired job mobility than whites (eight out of eleven).

18. I would like to point out that whites were equally likely to define themselves as rebellious as African-Americans (six out of eleven and five out of nine, respectively).

Chapter 4. The Organizing Campaigns at Bob's Grocery Stores and Geofelt Manufacturing

1. Ironically, by the next Christmas BGS had been successfully organized by the union and yet the store still remained open on Christmas Day. To make matters worse, BGS made all employees work at least a few hours rather than just those who volunteered as they had the previous Christmas. Workers were upset about the situation. As one worker explained: "We were told at a meeting that only workers with lowest seniority had to work, but Bob's got around that by making everyone work. And the people that volunteered got better schedules. That made me mad. The whole thing made me mad. I worked 9:30 to 6:00 on Christmas Day. I thought I'd never have to work Christmas again."

2. The Comprehensive Campaign was done to bypass an election, and the cards collected by the organizers during the BGS campaign were used to directly solicit union recognition from the company.

3. Organizers admitted that the union rarely gets involved in campaigns in which the company is financially insecure. If the company folds soon after the campaign election, not only is the recent expenditure wasted, but the union often gets blamed for business failure.

4. The union commonly asks management for union recognition before beginning an expensive and time-consuming organizing campaign.

5. Their research was done independently from one another.

6. Half of the members were white and half were African-American. Among the white committee members was one woman.

7. Two of the five workers not active in the prounion campaign were committee members in the antiunion campaign. I discuss this more below.

8. Four of the fifteen people I interviewed were committee members, so they also planned strategy. Besides the four committee members, three additional people drove around with the organizer to make house calls and helped plan strategy during the campaign.

9. Two of the three women in the plant were in the antiunion campaign. The third woman was on the prounion committee.

Chapter 6. The Contract Period and Beyond: Activism and Efficacy Among Workers

1. Of the five workers, one came from each of the four technicians' shifts and the fifth was from the shipping department. The lab and maintenance declined representation on the committee. Although white workers from the different shifts (except

shipping) ran for the positions, the workforce chose a majority of African-American employees—four African-Americans and one white.

2. This was the same meeting that I had also attended, described earlier in the chapter.

3. Three of the satisfied workers were African-American and two were white.

Bibliography

AFL-CIO. 1985. "The Changing Situation of Workers and Their Unions." *Committee on the Evolution of Work.* A Report of AFL-CIO, February.

AFL-CIO, Department of Organizing. 1989. *AFL-CIO Organizing Survey: 1986–87 NLRB Elections.* Washington, DC: AFL-CIO. Mimeo, February.

AFL-CIO. *The Blitz: A Manual for Organizers on How to Run Fast-Paced Pre-petition Campaigns.* Washington, DC: AFL-CIO.

Babbie, Earl. 1995. *The Practice of Social Research, Seventh Edition.* Belmont, CA: Wadsworth.

Bachrach, Peter. 1967. *The Theory of Democratic Elitism: A Critique.* Boston: Little, Brown.

Bachrach, Peter, and Arhey Botwinick. 1992. *Power and Empowerment: A Radical Theory of Participatory Democracy.* Philadelphia: Temple University Press.

Banks, Andy, and Jack Metzgar. 1989. "Participating in Management: Union Organizing on a New Terrain." *Labor Research Review* 14: 1–58.

Barbash, Jack. 1948. *Labor Unions in Action: The Study of the Mainsprings of Unionism.* New York: Harper and Brothers.

Barber, Benjamin R. 1984. *Strong Democracy: Participatory Politics for a New Age.* Berkeley: University of California Press.

Barkin, Solomon. 1992. "Organizing for the '90s." *LRA's Economic Notes* 60, no. 1: 12.

Benson, Herman. 1986. "The Fight for Union Democracy." In *Unions in Transition: Entering the Second Century,* ed. Seymour Martin Lipset, 323–370. San Francisco: ICS.

Bentham, Jeremy. [1823] 1948. *The Principles of Morals and Legislation.* New York: Hafner.

Bernstein, Paul. 1976. *Workplace Democratization: Its Internal Dynamics.*

Ohio: Comparative Administration Research Institute, distributed by Kent State University Press.

Block, Richard, and Benjamin Wolkinson. 1986. "Delay in the Union Election Campaign Revisited." In *Advances in Industrial and Labor Relations: A Research Annual,* eds. David B. Lipsky and David Lewin, 42–81. Greenwich, CT: JAI.

Blum, Albert A. 1993. "Towards Industrial Democracy." *Contemporary Review* 263: 120–26.

Blumberg, Paul. 1968. *Industrial Democracy: The Sociology of Participation.* London: Constable.

Bluestone, Barry, and Irving Bluestone. 1992. *Negotiating the Future: A Labor Perspective on American Business.* New York: Basic.

Bonacich, Edna. 1972. "A Theory of Ethnic Antagonism: The Split Labor Market." *American Sociological Review* 37: 547–59.

Brecher, Jeremy, and Tim Costello. 1996. "A 'New Labor Movement' in the Shell of the Old?" *Labor Research Review* 24: 5–25.

Bronfenbrenner, Kate. 1997. "The Role of Union Strategies in NLRB Certification Elections." *Industrial and Labor Relations Review* 50, no. 2: 195–211.

———. 1994. "Employer Behavior in Certification Elections and First-Contract Campaigns: Implications for Labor Law Reform." In *Restoring the Promises of American Labor Law,* eds. Sheldon Friedman, Richard Hurd, Rudolph Oswald, and Ronald Seeber, 75–89. Ithaca, NY: ILR.

———. 1993. "Seeds of Resurgence: Successful Union Strategies for Winning Certification Elections and First Contracts in the 1980s and Beyond." Ph.D. dissertation, Cornell University.

Bronfenbrenner, Kate, and Tom Juravich. 1996. "It Takes More Than Housecalls: Organizing to Win with a Comprehensive Union-Building Strategy." Paper read at the AFL-CIO/Cornell Joint Union/ University Research Conference on Organizing, Washington, DC, March-April.

Butler, Margaret. 1991. "Organizing for Everything We Do: CWA at AT&T and US West." *Labor Research Review* 18, no. 1: 7–18.

Chacko, Thomas. 1985. "Member Participation in Union Activities: Perceptions of Union Priorities, Performances and Satisfaction." *Journal of Labor Research* 6, no. 4: 363–73.

Chaison, Gary. 1986. *When Unions Merge.* Washington, DC: Lexington Books.

Chatak, Elmer. 1991. "A Unionist's Perspective on the Future of American Unions." *Journal of Labor Research* 12, no. 4: 327–32.

Chinoy, Ely. 1955. *Automobile Workers and the American Dream.* Boston: Beacon.

Cole, G.D.H. 1928. *Self-Government in Industry*. London: Macmillan.
———. 1920. *Social Theory*. New York: Frederick A. Stokes.
Cook, Terrence E., and Patrick M. Morgan. 1971. *Participatory Democracy*. San Francisco: Canfield.
Cooper, Terry L. 1980. "Bureaucracy and Community Organizations: The Metamorphosis of a Relationship." *Administration and Society* 11, no. 4: 411–44.
Cornfield, Daniel. 1986. "Declining Union Membership in the Post–World War II Era: The United Furniture Workers of America, 1939–1982." *American Journal of Sociology* 91, no. 5: 1112–53.
Cornfield, Daniel, Hilquias Filho, and Bang Chun. 1990. "Household, Work, and Labor Activism: Gender Differences in the Determinants of Union Membership Participation." *Work and Occupations* 17, no. 2: 131–151.
Cornfield, Daniel, and Randy Hodson. 1993. "Labor Activism and Community: Causes and Consequences of Social Integration in Labor Unions." *Social Science Quarterly* 74, no. 3: 590–602.
Cornfield, Daniel, and Mark Leners. 1989. "Unionization in the Rural South: Regional Patterns of Industrialization and the Process of Union Organizing." *Research in Rural Sociology and Development*, 4: 137–152.
Craft, James A., and Marian M. Extejt. 1983. "New Strategies in Union Organizing." *Journal of Labor Research* 4, no. 1: 19–32.
Craypo, Charles, and Bruce Nissen. 1993. *Grand Designs: The Impact of Corporate Strategies on Workers, Unions, and Communities*. Ithaca, NY: ILR.
Derber, Charles, and William Schwartz. 1983. "Toward a Theory of Worker Participation." *Sociological Inquiry* 53, no. 1: 61–78.
Dickens, William. 1983. "The Effect of Company Campaigns on Certification Elections: Law and Reality Once Again." *Industrial and Labor Relations Review* 36: 560–75.
Dickens, William, and Jonathan Leonard. 1985. "Accounting for the Decline in Union Membership, 1950–1980." *Industrial and Labor Relations Review* 38, no. 3: 323–34.
Domhoff, G. William. 1990. *The Power Elite and the State: How Policy Is Made in America*. Hawthorne, NY: Aldine de Gruyter.
Edwards, Richard. 1979. *Contested Terrain: The Transformation of the Workplace in the Twentieth Century*. New York: Basic.
Elden, J. Maxwell. 1981. "Political Efficacy at Work: The Connection Between More Autonomous Forms of Workplace Organization and a More Participatory Politics." *American Political Science Review* 75 (March): 43–58.
Fantasia, Rick. 1988. *Cultures of Solidarity: Consciousness, Action, and Contemporary American Workers*. Berkeley: University of California Press.

Fantasia, Rick, Dan Clawson, and Gregory Graham. 1988. "A Critical View of Worker Participation in American Industry." *Work and Occupations* 15, no. 4: 468–88.

Fletcher, Richard. 1970. "Trade Union Democracy—Structural Factors." In *Trade Union Register,* ed. Ken Coates, Tony Topham, and Michael Barratt Brown, 73–85. London: Merlin.

Freeman, Richard. 1985. "Why Are Unions Faring Poorly in NLRB Representation Elections?" In *Challenges and Choices Facing American Labor,* ed. Thomas Kochan, 45–64. Cambridge, MA: MIT Press.

Freeman, Richard, and Morris M. Kleiner. 1990. "Employer Behavior in the Face of Union Organizing Drives." *Industrial and Labor Relations Review* 43, no. 4: 351–65.

Freeman, Richard, and James Medoff. 1984. "Trade Unions and Productivity: Some New Evidence on an Old Issue." *Annals of the American Academy of Political and Social Science* 473 (May): 149–64.

Gamson, William. 1992. *Talking Politics.* New York: Cambridge University Press.

Gittel, Marilyn. 1980. *Limits to Citizen Participation: The Decline of Community Organizations.* Beverly Hills: Sage.

Goffman, Erving. 1974. *Frame Analysis: An Essay on the Organization of Experience.* Cambridge, MA: Harvard University Press.

Goldfield, Michael. 1989. "Worker Insurgency, Radical Organization, and New Deal Labor Legislation." *American Political Science Review* 83, no. 4: 1257–81.

———. 1987. *The Decline of Organized Labor in the United States.* Chicago: University of Chicago Press.

Gouldner, Alvin. 1954. *Wildcat Strike.* Yellow Springs, OH: Antioch.

Greenberg, Edward. 1986. *Workplace Democracy: The Political Effects of Participation.* Ithaca, NY: Cornell University Press.

Gross, James A. 1974. *The Making of the National Labor Relations Board.* Albany: State University of New York Press.

Halle, David. 1984. *America's Working Man: Work, Home and Politics Among Blue Collar Property Owners.* Chicago: University of Chicago Press.

Hathaway, Dale. 1993. *Can Workers Have a Voice? The Politics of Deindustrialization in Pittsburgh.* University Park, PA: Pennsylvania State University Press.

Heckscher, Charles. 1988. *The New Unionism: Employee Involvement in the Changing Corporation.* New York: Basic.

Herberg, Will. 1943. "Bureaucracy and Democracy in Labor Unions." *Antioch Review* 3: 405–17.

Hodson, Randy. 1995. "Cohesion or Conflict? Race, Solidarity, and Resistance in the Workplace." *Research in the Sociology of Work* 5: 135–59.

Hodson, Randy, Sandy Welsh, Sabine Rieble, Cheryl Jamison, and Sean Creighton. 1993. "Is Worker Solidarity Undermined by Autonomy and Participation?" *American Sociological Review* 58, no. 3: 398–416.

Hogler, Raymond L., and Guillermo J. Grenier. 1992. *Employee Participation and Labor Law in the American Workplace.* New York: Quorum.

Howley, John. 1990. "Justice for Janitors: The Challenge of Organizing in Contract Services." *Labor Research Review* 15: 61–71.

Hurd, Richard W. 1976. "New Deal Labor Policy and the Containment of Radical Union Activity." *Review of Radical Political Economics* 8, no. 3: 32–43.

Hurd, Richard W., and Adrienne McElwain. 1988. "Organizing Clerical Workers: Determinants of Success." *Industrial and Labor Relations Review* 41, no. 3: 360–73.

Hurd, Richard, and William Rouse. 1989. "Progressive Union Organizing: The SEIU Justice for Janitors Campaign: Competing Explanations for the Decline in Union Organizing Success." *Review of Radical Political Economics* 21, no. 3: 70–75.

Hurd, Rick. 1986. "Building the Ranks: Bottom-up Organizing: HERE in New Haven and Boston." *Labor Research Review* 8 (Spring): 5–19.

Jarley, Paul, and Cheryl L. Maranto. 1990. "Union Corporate Campaigns: An Assessment." *Industrial and Labor Relations Review* 43, no. 5: 505–524.

Johnston, Paul. 1994. *Success While Others Fail: Social Movement Unionism.* Ithaca, NY: ILR.

Jones, Mary Harris. [1925] 1972. *The Autobiography of Mother Jones,* ed. Mary Field Parton. Chicago: Charles H. Kerr.

Kerr, Clark, and Abraham Siegel. 1954. "Propensity to Strike: An International Comparison." In *Industrial Conflict,* ed. A. Kornhauser. New York: McGraw Hill.

Kochan, Thomas A., Harry C. Katz, and Robert B. McKersie. 1986. *The Transformation of American Industrial Relations.* New York: Basic.

Lawler, Edward III, Susan Mohrmann, and Gerald Ledford Jr. 1992. *Employee Involvement and Total Quality Management: Practices and Results in Fortune 1000 Companies.* San Francisco: Jossey-Bass.

Lawson, J.W. 1977. *How to Meet the Challenge of the Union Organizer.* Chicago: Dartnell Corporation.

Leggett, John C. 1968. *Class, Race, and Labor: Working-Class Consciousness in Detroit.* New York: Oxford University Press.

Lester, Richard A. 1958. *As Unions Mature: An Analysis of the Evolution of American Unionism.* Princeton, NJ: Princeton University Press.

Levitt, Martin Jay. 1993. *Confessions of a Union Buster.* New York: Crown.

Lincoln, James, and Arne Kalleberg. 1990. *Culture, Control and Commitment: A Study of Work Organization and Work Attitudes in the United States and Japan.* New York: Cambridge University Press.

Lipset, Seymour, Martin Trow, and James Coleman. 1956. *Union Democracy: The Internal Politics of the International Typographical Union.* Garden City, NY: Anchor.

Locke, John. 1777. *The Works of John Locke.* London: Printed for W. Strahan. 3rd ed.

Lopreato, Joseph, and Lawrence Hazelrigg. 1972. *Class, Conflict, and Mobility: Theories and Studies of Class Structure.* San Francisco: Chandler.

Mansbridge, Jane J. 1980. *Beyond Adversary Democracy.* New York: Basic.

Marx, Karl, and Friedrich Engels. [1888] 1963. *The Communist Manifesto.* New York: Russell and Russell.

Mason, Ronald. 1982. *Participatory and Workplace Democracy: A Theoretical Development in Critique of Liberalism.* Carbondale, IL: Southern Illinois University Press.

McDonald, Joseph, and Donald Clelland. 1984. ''Textile Workers and Union Sentiment.'' *Social Forces* 63, no. 2: 502–21.

Metzgar, Jack. 1991. ''Let's Get Moving! Organizing for the 90's.'' *Labor Research Review* 18: 83–91.

Michels, Robert. [1915] 1962. *Political Parties: A Sociological Study of the Oligarchical Tendencies of Modern Democracy.* Translated by Eden and Cedar Paul. Gloucester, MA: Peter Smith.

Moody, Kim. 1988. *An Injury to All: The Decline of American Labor.* New York: Verso.

Moos, Rudolf H. 1986. ''Work as a Human Context.'' In *Psychology of Work* 9–48. Washington, DC: American Sociological Association.

Mosca, Gaetano. 1939. *The Ruling Class.* New York: McGraw-Hill.

Mowday, Richard T., Lymand W. Porter, and Richard M. Steers. 1982. *Employee-Organization Linkages: The Psychology of Commitment, Absenteeism and Turnover.* New York: Academic.

Northrup, Herbert. 1991. '' 'New' Union Approaches to Membership Decline: Reviving the Policies of the 1920s?'' *Journal of Labor Research* 12, no. 4: 333–47.

Oppenheim, Lisa. 1991. Introduction to ''Let's Get Moving! Organizing for the 90's.'' *Labor Research Review* 18: 45–60.

Parker, Mike, and Jane Slaughter. 1988. *Choosing Sides: Unions and the Team Concept.* Boston: South End.

Pateman, Carole. 1970. *Participation and Democratic Theory.* London: Cambridge University Press.

Perry, Charles R. 1987. *Union Corporate Campaigns.* Philadelphia: Industrial Research Unit of the Wharton School.

Peterson, Richard B., Thomas W. Lee, and Barbara Finnegan. 1992. "Strategies and Tactics in Union Organizing Campaigns." *Industrial Relations* 31, no. 2: 370–81.

Prosten, Richard. 1978. "The Longest Season: Union Organizing in the Last Decade, a/k/a: How Come One Team Has to Play with Its Shoelaces Tied Together?" *Industrial Relations Research Association Series,* Proceedings of the Thirty-First Annual Meeting, August 29–31: 240–49.

Robinson, J. Gregg. 1988. "American Unions in Decline: Problems and Prospects." *Critical Sociology* 15, no. 1: 33–56.

Roby, Pamela, and Lynet Uttal. 1988. "Trade Union Stewards: Handling Union, Family and Employment Responsibilities." In *Women and Work: An Annual Review,* eds. Barbara Gutek, Ann Stromberg, and Laurie Larwood. Newbury Park, CA: Sage.

Rostov, Stanley David. 1948. "Factors Affecting the Success of Union Organizing Efforts: As Seen in a Local Campaign of the International Ladies' Garment Workers' Union." Master's thesis, University of Illinois.

Rothschild, Joyce, and J. Allen Whitt. 1986. *The Cooperative Workplace: Potentials and Dilemmas of Organizational Democracy and Participation.* Cambridge, MA: Cambridge University Press.

Rubin, Beth. 1986. "Class Struggle American Style: Union, Strikes and Wages." *American Sociological Review* 51 (October): 618–31.

Sartori, Giovanni. 1965. *Democratic Theory.* New York: Praeger.

Saposs, David. 1971. *Communism in American Unions.* New York: McGraw Hill.

Schumpeter, Joseph. 1942. *Capitalism, Socialism and Democracy,* 3rd ed. New York: Harper Torchbooks.

Sexton, Patricia Cayo. 1991. *The War on Labor and the Left: Understanding America's Unique Conservatism.* Boulder, CO: Westview.

Shaiken, Harley. 1984. *Work Transfer: Automation and Labor in the Computer Age.* New York: Holt, Rinehart, and Winston.

Shaiken, Harley, Stephen Herzenberg, and Sarah Kuhn. 1986. "The Work Process Under More Flexible Production." *Industrial Relations* 25, no. 2: 167–83.

Shostak, Arthur. 1991. *Robust Unionism: Innovations in the Labor Movement.* Ithaca, NY: ILR.

Simmons, Louise. 1994. *Organizing in Hard Times: Labor and Neighborhoods in Hartford.* Philadelphia: Temple University Press.

Sockell, Donna, and John Thomas Delaney. 1987. "Union Organizing and the Reagan NLRB." *Contemporary Policy Issues* 5, no. 4: 28–45.

Snow, David, Burke Rochford, Steven Worden, and Robert Benford. 1986. "Frame Alignment Processes, Micromobilization, and Movement Participation." *American Sociological Review* 51, no. 4: 464–81.

Stepan-Norris, Judith, and Maurice Zeitlin. 1996. "Insurgency, Radicalism, and Democracy in America's Industrial Unions." *Social Forces* 75, no. 1: 1–32.

———. 1991. " 'Red' Unions and 'Bourgeois Contracts'?" *American Journal of Sociology* 96: 1151–1200.

Strauss, George. 1991. "Union Democracy." In *State of the Unions,* eds. George Strauss, Daniel G. Gallagher, and Jack Fiorito, 201–36. Wisconsin: Industrial Relations Research Association Press.

Taplin, Ian. 1990. "The Contradictions of Business Unionism and the Decline of Organized Labour." *Economic and Industrial Democracy* 11, no. 2: 249–78.

Ventriss, Curtis, and Robert Pecorella. 1984. "Community Participation and Modernization: A Reexamination of Political Choices." *Public Administration Review* 44: 224–31.

Voos, Paula. 1984. "Trends in Union Organizing Expenditures, 1953–1977." *Industrial and Labor Relations Review* 38, no. 1: 52–63.

Voss, Kim. 1993. *The Making of American Exceptionalism.* Ithaca, NY: Cornell University Press.

Voss, Kim, and Rachel Sherman. 1997. "Putting the 'Move' Back in Labor Movement: Tactical Innovation and Contemporary Labor Unions." Paper read at the annual meeting of the American Sociological Association, Toronto, Canada, August.

Walker, Jack L. 1966. "A Critique of the Elitist Theory of Democracy." *American Political Science Review* 60, no. 2: 285–95.

Walsh, John. 1993. *Supermarkets Transformed: Understanding Organizational and Technological Innovations.* New Brunswick, NJ: Rutgers University Press.

Weiler, Paul. 1990. *Governing the Workplace: The Future of Labor and Employment Law.* Cambridge, MA: Harvard University Press.

Waldinger, Roger, Chris Erickson, Ruth Milkman, Daniel J.B. Mitchell, Abel Valenzuela, Kent Wong, and Maurice Zeitlin. 1997. "Justice for Janitors." *Dissent* (Winter): 37–44.

Zald, Mayer, and John D. McCarthy. 1987. *Social Movements in an Organizational Society: Collected Essays.* New Brunswick, NJ: Transaction Books.

Zetka, Jr., James. 1992a. "Work Organization and Wildcat Strikes in the U.S. Automobile Industry, 1946–1963." *American Sociological Review* 57 (April): 214–26.

———. 1992b. "Mass Production, Automation and Work-Group Solidarity in the Post-World War II Automobile Industry." *Work and Occupations* 19, no. 3: 255–71.

Zingraff, Rhonda, and Michael Schulman. 1984. "Social Bases of Class Consciousness: A Study of Southern Textile Workers with a Comparison by Race." *Social Forces* 63, no. 1: 98–116.

Index